CLOSING
THE BOOK

TRAVELS IN LIFE, LOSS, AND LITERATURE

JOELLE RENSTROM

Joelle Renstrom

Pelekinesis

CLOSING THE BOOK: Travels in Life, Loss, and Literature
by Joelle Renstrom

ISBN: 978-1-938349-24-9
eISBN: 978-1-938349-26-3
Library of Congress Control Number: 2015936091

"A Sort of Homecoming" was published in *Barely South Review* (Sept 2012)

"Letters to Ray Bradbury" was published in *Konundrum* Magazine (2009)

"Making Luck" was published in the *Paradigm Journal* (Sept 2010)

"Fighting the Sunday Blues with Albert Camus" was published in *Briarpatch*

(Sept 2009) under the name "Freedom and Absurdity in the Classroom."

"How I Spent My Free Will" was published in the *Minnetonka Review*

(Winter 2011)

"Finding Fathers" was published in *Ducts* Magazine (Dec 2010)

Layout and Book Design by Mark Givens

First Pelekinesis Printing 2015

For information:
Pelekinesis, 112 Harvard Ave #65, Claremont, CA 91711 USA

www.pelekinesis.com

Closing the Book:
Travels in Life, Loss, and Literature

Joelle Renstrom

Praise for Joelle Renstrom

"Joelle Renstrom brought back my grief at my own father's death, and finally, in significant ways, allowed me to move past it. She is a wise and honest writer, the most thoughtful of travel companions, and a brilliant interpreter of the ways life and literature connect. As I read, I found myself wishing she had been my teacher--then realized, gratefully, upon closing the cover, that she had been."

Eileen Pollack, author of *The Only Woman in the Room: Why Science Is Still a Boys' Club*

"Many of us use literature as a guide, an inspiration, a support in times of trouble and need. Travel serves some of the same purposes—as an escape into otherness, a way of learning, a standard for comparison with the world we live in ordinarily. But few of us have the knack Joelle Renstrom has of writing about how life, literature, and travel intersect and feed off one another. *Closing the Book* is both deeply personal and at the same time open and welcoming enough that we can find ourselves in these pages and learn something there about loss, grief and growth."

Richard Tillinghast, author of *Finding Ireland* and *An Armchair Traveller's History of Istanbul*

Closing the Book:
Travels in Life, Loss, and Literature

Joelle Renstrom

List of Essays *(and corresponding literature)*

For my dad
for whom death is no match.
I'll see you in Paris.

A Sort of Homecoming

"We know what no other animal knows,
that we must die."
Don DeLillo, *White Noise*

Friday June 2, 2006, 12:34 PM Pacific Standard Time. I'm taking my lunch break on the Cecil Green lawn at the University of British Columbia, where I currently work and have just finished graduate school. It's a perfect day—seventy-five degrees and sunny, the ocean lapping gently in the background, flowers flanking the lawn. The smell of cut grass.

Last night, my dad was admitted into the hospital with what his doctor thought was pneumonia. He'd been uncharacteristically sick with a cold for weeks— he'd even opted out of three consecutive Sunday golf outings, which was unheard of—and antibiotics weren't working. His being in the hospital was disconcerting, but no one seemed particularly worried. These things happened. They'd be doing a chest x-ray this morning, just to be sure. Mom was supposed to call me to let me know everything was okay.

I check my watch again. It's 3:37 in Michigan. The ring echoes in my ear and then cuts to the answering machine when I try Mom and Dad's house the second time. Like a horse that senses a coming storm, this disquiet has me wanting to fidget and stomp. I call my mom's cell. She picks up but doesn't say hello. In a strange, strangled voice she says, "It's not pneumonia."

This is the moment that divides my life into before and after.

* * *

The next morning, unable to think about anything except getting there, I fly to Kalamazoo, feeling as though untold horrible things could be happening while I am unreachable on an airplane, but that they somehow can't if I'm there.

24 hours ago I debated whether to put milk in my coffee; 22 hours ago I installed new file management software on my computer at work; 20 hours ago I was thinking about trying a new Mexican restaurant for dinner, about margaritas with extra salt.

Now, I'm thinking about the man who recently died on a Greyhound bus after his seatmate, a perfect stranger, sawed his head off.

I'm contemplating plane crashes, the awareness of

imminent death. The stretch and suspension of that moment before gravity and reality take hold. Once when I was biking down Second Avenue in New York a van door swung open and I had just enough time to realize that I was going to hit it. But that's pretty small stuff; I still bike in rush hour traffic. This is more like driving a car off a cliff, that misleading airborne instant before the fall.

Successful crash landings are interesting. All those people barreling toward the termination of all future moments, their sudden acquaintance with fear and mortality and finality. And then, against whatever odds, they survive, their own deaths now something they know and have seen up close, their relationship with themselves and the world changed.

I think about whether successful crash landings are due to skill or luck, or some perfect combination of both. Whether we have what it takes to get to the ground alive.

* * *

I go straight to the hospital, where CT scans confirm stage four cancer that originated in the colon and spread to the liver and lungs. The oncologist's best guess is that the initial tumor started growing in Dad's colon six or seven years ago, shortly after his last colonoscopy. This news not only has significant and terrifying implications for the future, but it also changes the past. When Dad visited me while I lived in New York, when we saw plays on Broadway and walked across the Brooklyn Bridge and sat for six hours at the Belgian beer bar, he had cancer. All of these memories, milestones, and celebrations, these moments with no discernible darkness, were in fact hiding a fatal truth growing inside his body. I feel robbed in retrospect by the privilege of ignorance.

When I first walk into Dad's hospital room and see him lying there sprouting IVs, oxygen tubes in his nose, pulse oximeter on his finger, feet sticking out over the end of the bed, I am struck immediately by a sense of déjà vu. As I rush to hug him, the movement is accompanied by a sense of practice, as though this is a scene I've played in before. Perhaps it's because this is the stuff of the saddest stories, the images we see and fear will one day resemble a moment in our lives. I stop myself from indulging the memory that haunts the edges of my mind and, tucked into Dad's hollowed chest, I try to orient myself toward the future, toward what we need to do for the rest of today, for tomorrow, for the rest of Dad's life.

"This is a good excuse to get you home for a visit, eh?" he says. A Detroit Tigers game plays on mute in the background, and every now and then he glances toward it to check the score. He says we shouldn't panic just yet, and we oblige, at least on the surface. We wait to fall apart.

The oncologist wants to start Dad on chemotherapy immediately and is checking on some clinical trials. The surgeon will be in soon for a consult. Things are bad, but it's unclear what that means, whether things can get less bad. Maddening as it is, the ambiguity prevents us from collapsing. The world tips wildly, poised to spin off its axis like a deranged top. But it hasn't happened yet. Uncertainty means that not all hope is lost, and we hold onto hope in everything— the way we watch television and get invested in stolen bases, the way we meet the eyes of the doctors and nurses, the purposeful way our bodies move toward attainable goals and reasonable ambitions, the grip of our shoes on the waxy linoleum of the hospital floor.

The house is changed; it's strange not to hear his footsteps, not to see his head, the soft grey hair sticking out over the back of the recliner in the living room. No snores thundering through the wall at night. I check the freezer for ice cream. When I grab for a spoon, the phonebook and pens and Post-its are in the drawer where the silverware used to be and all the utensils are in the drawer under the phone. That the spoons aren't where they're supposed to be throws me, at once a clear and ominous metaphor.

I walk around the house in my socks, quiet, as though someone sick is sleeping. My old bedroom is now Dad's office. His laptop is open on the desk. Stacks of legal pads with notes written in red felt pen in his scratching sloping hand. Textbooks, political paraphernalia, family photos. The ticket stubs from when we saw Tori Amos at Radio City Music Hall together, his mementos overlapping with mine. I'd rather he be the one to inhabit this space.

I walk into my parents' bedroom. The last time Dad was in here, no one knew he had cancer.

On the shelf above his bed, I see the copy of Don DeLillo's *White Noise* that I bought him a couple years ago. For birthdays and Christmas, Dad always asked me to give him books and music that I particularly liked—this is how Dad developed a liking for both Tori Amos and trance music. He said he appreciated DeLillo's writing, but didn't know quite what to make of my being so wild about a book about death. Now I feel a cramp in my side, a sharp guilt pang for having put into his life a book fixated on both the abstractions and the actualities of death.

I grab the book from the shelf roughly, as though

it has introduced a toxic element into my dad's life. As I thumb through it, I decide to read it again—it's been seven or eight years, and I'm curious whether I'll still love this book and whether it has anything to teach me that would have been lost on me before.

In the beginning of *White Noise*, Jack Gladney and his wife Babette, and even their three teenage kids, are keenly aware of their mortality, if only in a fairly abstract way. It's as though they all sense that death hovers everywhere, including around them, but it hasn't yet landed. Babette lives in such terror of that moment that she goes to extremes to obtain an experimental and dangerous psycho-pharmaceutical drug designed to dull the fear. But nothing can, because nothing can prevent death. This idea is reinforced in the book when the spilling of an incredibly poisonous chemical triggers a "toxic event," a huge dark cloud that floats around and gives chase, full of rain and wind that kill. As they evacuate town, Jack fills up the car with gas, exposing himself directly to the toxins for about two minutes. Later, in the shelter, a doctor tells Jack that the exposure will kill him in roughly 30 years. Even though 30 years is a relatively long time, the doctor pulls death out of the ether and pins it on Jack, guaranteeing that Jack's awareness of his mortality will sharpen into something deadly and insidious—an active watching of the clock and listening for the bomb that ticks inside him. The morning of the toxic event, Jack had woken up believing that he'd built a safe home with a wonderful and comforting wife who takes him to her breast each night, a house packed with kids so intelligent and curious and fierce that they cannot possibly be mortal. We all know that death is out there somewhere, but like most of us, Jack believes that death is busy attending to more pressing matters elsewhere. Once Jack learns that death is watching him, and not from afar, it infiltrates his safe spaces.

I wonder how Dad felt when he got diagnosed, the moment he realized that despite clean and healthy living, he was going to die much sooner than later. The moment he realized that death was in his house, his bedroom, in him, that it had been for years. I wonder whether it would be better to get hit by a bus or to die suddenly in a freak accident than to realize that death had bypassed the best home alarm system, family, and lifestyle and had invaded a body that was supposed to belong to its owner.

In *White Noise,* déjà vu is a side effect of exposure to the toxic chemical, a side effect of exposure to death. I think about my déjà vu in the hospital room, about one particular side effect of the moment that changed everything. Mine wasn't a reaction to a chemical. For my graduate thesis, I wrote a novel in which one of the protagonists was a girl roughly my age; naturally, we had quite a bit in common. When, at a turning point in the book, I needed something devastating to happen to her, I asked myself what would be the most devastating thing that could happen to me.

So the character's dad has an aneurysm during a welcome home party for her and she spends the next two weeks watching him die. I cried as I wrote those scenes—I imagined holding my dad's hand as he lay comatose in a hospital bed. What I would say, how I would lean over him, trying to find his breath, wondering if the passing over was at hand or if he was already gone.

I projected into my novel the most devastating thing I could imagine, and then it happened. Even though I keep telling myself it's a coincidence, I don't want to touch the book ever again—it's tainted, a talisman of death. Logically this makes no sense—the tumor started growing in Dad's colon long before the book was a glint in my eye. Yet I can't seem to still the sense that my writing provided another pathway for death to reach my dad.

And I can't stop wondering what it means—what

the past two years of my life mean—if the only significant and cultivated aspect of my life that I can bring with me from Vancouver is now as good as dead.

Even though Dad's diagnosis has changed everything for me and for the rest of my family, it appears that the world at large hasn't changed, unlike in *White Noise*, unlike after 9/11. At the time, 9/11 made me think of *White Noise*, with its aftermath of smoggy clouds and debris and chemicals floating in the air. Unlike with 9/11, Dad's diagnosis alienates me from the rest of the world and from almost everyone I know because this is a private tragedy; it requires explanation. Even then, some people don't get it. One of my friends says something like, "I know what you're going through. The same thing happened to us last year when my grandfather died." And I want to say no, this isn't the same. Your grandfather was 85. His death, while certainly sad, is natural—old people die. Grandfathers die. It's not the same as a healthy 63-year-old man being besieged by cancer.

Even the friends who weep with me can hang up the phone, disconnect from this, and go on with their lives. They must breathe sighs of relief—I'll admit I've done it before—that this isn't happening to them. Of course, this happens to almost everyone sooner or later. I'm not the only person whose father has gotten sick; people have lost fathers at far younger ages and in more horrible ways. There are people against whom far greater injustices have been done— the sick kids I see haunting the hospital hallways remind me of that every day. I know my anger is disproportionate, that I'm avoiding people I like and perhaps need. My life has suddenly diverged from most of the other lives I know, and the thought of trying to explain all of this makes me want to throw up.

The greatest comfort for Jack and Babette is spending time with their four-year-old son, Wilder, because "he doesn't know he's going to die. He doesn't know death at all." Wilder becomes like Buddha, both lucky and enlightened. "You cherish this simpleton blessing of his, this exemption from harm. You want to get close to him, touch him, look at him, breathe him in. How lucky he is. A cloud of unknowing, an omnipotent little person. The child is everything, the adult nothing."

The closest thing I have to Wilder is my cat, Zola, whose rusty purr is one of the only things that hasn't changed, that still offers comfort. But at this moment, she's back in Vancouver, unaware of death, unaware of everything except perhaps, in fleeting moments here and there, my absence. I find myself wanting to be Wilder's age again, a little ball of wonder. When I would go to sleep before eight pm, when all I ate was macaroni and cheese, when Dad made me a "world's greatest muckraker" button after I jumped in his pile of leaves.

* * *

After conferencing with the hospitalist, generalist, internist, and surgeon, the oncologist tells us that Dad is terminal. There is a treatment protocol, including a clinical trial, that could extend Dad's life, but he will never not have cancer. Then they say he has six months to two years left, which shakes us down to our bones. A few weeks later, we'd give anything for six months.

That night I go to my brother's house to devise a game plan. In a few days Dad will leave the hospital. He'll have six hours of chemotherapy every Wednesday, and every Friday he'll get an immune-boosting shot. Then there's the regimen of pills, some of which are supposed to mitigate the side effects of the treatment. We know that Dad returning home means everything about life at home will change, too. He'll need oxygen tanks, special food, new clothes. Someone has to do all the things my dad used to do around the house. As though we can manage this, my brother and I make a spreadsheet.

At some point during our strategizing, the phone rings. It's a friend of my brother's who, in the process of moving, is about to get rid of his cat carrier. My brother says, "We already have a cat carrier, thanks," and in that moment we look at each other and I mouth, "I'll take it." This is the first time I've said out loud that I'm moving back.

A couple days later, I head back to Vancouver to wrap everything up. Leaving Kalamazoo, even if only for a couple of weeks, is excruciating—what will happen when I'm not here? Among other things, my dad will return home to reoccupy the space he's lived in for the last 27 years, except this time, he'll already be a ghost. The house in which I grew up will never look or feel like it did when I was a child, when, like Wilder, I lived in the before, blissfully innocent of the after.

* * *

Vancouver too has changed. When I left, it was my home. I had a new Masters degree, a novel I was planning to send to agents, a boyfriend, an apartment, friends, and a job I actually liked. Now, that life is a faint shadow.

I give notice at work and wrap up projects, explain to my landlord why I have to break my lease, give to friends or put on Craig's List almost everything I own. Strangers parade through my apartment, examining my furniture, bouncing on the couch, trying out my appliances, stacking up my books and clothes. Strangers will incorporate my things into their lives— soon someone will ride my bike around town, someone will water my plants and grow them on a south-facing windowsill. Someone will cook with my pots and pans and then eat around my kitchen table.

My boyfriend and I know that this is the end of us, given that it's unlikely we'll live in the same city, or country, anytime soon; he's not legal to work in the States and neither of us wants an indefinite long-distance relationship. This is yet another aftershock; they seem to reach everywhere, growing legs, radiating, shifting pieces of my life that I thought were solid. Under the circumstances, I have no regrets about moving back, but I can't forget that in the before world, this is something I would never have considered doing. I feel as if I've been shoved backwards, away from the places and things I saw on the horizon; I won't be passing *Go* for a long time.

Three weeks later, I ride through Vancouver on the way to the airport knowing it will be a while before I see the city again, that this may be the last time I ride in my boyfriend Eric's car. My cat wails in the back seat, pressing her forehead against the door of the cat carrier. I feel as though I'm leaving an iteration of myself behind—one that I'm only now realizing was incredibly fortunate.

After the toxic cloud dissipates, Jack and Babette realize that things can't go back to the way they were before the cloud, that their lives have become meaningless rituals, pathetic recreations. Jack becomes prone to nostalgia for his old life, for the time before his acute awareness of his incipient death. Suddenly, the world of yesterday, even with its gamma rays and microwaves and x-rays, its indefatigable white noise, the hum of a life force greater than those who invented it, feels idyllic and, in retrospect, woefully underappreciated. Jack struggles to connect the world he used to inhabit with the new one; even when the changes are as difficult to detect as the chemical in Jack's system, they are there nonetheless, growing like a tumor.

Before Dad got sick, visiting Kalamazoo and the icons of my childhood was gratifying and indulgent— it stoked my appreciation for the people and places that shaped me. Now it feels as though I've gone back to my childhood home only to find it full of crumbling plaster and frayed wires; yet my only option is to stay there, trapped between desperate nostalgia and the rapidly darkening future.

* * *

The first thing I notice when I get back is the oxygen hub in the kitchen, a futuristic unit that looks like a squatting spaceship, humming as it recycles oxygen and dispenses it through a tube. The tube is like a leash—Dad is always at the other end, inhaling deeply through his nose. Once or twice the dog trips over the tube and yanks it, leaving Dad surprised and gasping. He's pale and tired and fades into the afternoons. When I put my arms around him, my fingers touch across his back. I can feel his ribs under my armpits, shuddering with breath.

The bathroom teems with special mouthwash, pill bottles, basins, the smell of the sick. As I get ready for bed on my first night back, I see the history of myself in the mirror. How many times I've stood here studying my own face, wetting down the cowlicks in my bangs, poking at my skin, peering up my nose, checking to see if my ears stick out, undulating my hips, practicing come hither looks, trying to see if my eyes and face really show what I'm thinking and feeling. When something big happened in my life, I'd always check the mirror to see if I looked any different, trying to determine whether my mom would be able to tell.

Feature for feature, the face I see in the mirror is mine; it matches up to the one in the photos that hang in the hallway outside, but it feels as though someone else is wearing it. I tilt my head, smile, frown, and bare my teeth with the curious sensation that I know this face, but I can't remember how or from where, like maybe I borrowed it a while ago from someplace that now escapes my mind.

No one else seems to be able to tell. I look like I've always looked, maybe a little thinner; we're all thinner. To everyone else, despite being unmistakably devastated, I seem to be the same sturdy person I've always been. That someone is walking around wearing my face is a piece of information that I carry quietly and dutifully, like a pebble in a shoe.

On my third day back Dad walks into my room as I'm sitting at the desk, typing on his laptop.

"I've kind of taken your room over," he says apologetically.

"It's fine," I say. "I'm glad you hang out in here." I swivel the chair. We both look around at the walls, at the combination of my relics and his, the overlapping of stories.

"Did I interrupt?" he asks. "Were you writing?"

"No," I say. "Just checking email."

He sits on the edge of the bed, looping the oxygen cord around his wrist, careful not to catch it on anything. "So, what's the status of your book?"

I sigh. "I don't know."

He breathes deeply, in through his nose and out his mouth. He doesn't say anything, waits.

"Want to hear something strange?" I ask.

He smiles. "Sure."

I tell him about the book, about the protagonist's dead dad.

He listens, hands resting on his knees, oxygen cord dangling between them. Every so often he nods slightly, as though to affirm that he's still with me. "Yeah," he says after I finish, "that's pretty strange. But the bottom line is that your book doesn't have anything to do with me being sick. I think you should keep working on it. And don't do anything foolish, like having the character's dad live."

I laugh, a burst of relief. "I'll keep that in mind. So you're not freaked out or upset by it?" As I say it, I realize that Dad hasn't freaked out about anything yet.

"Nah," he says. "I don't think I could ever be upset by anything you write."

I look at the cork board above the desk, where he has put up some of my poems with thumbtacks. "Could you be upset by something I decide not to write?"

He shakes his head. "Nope. You're the writer. You know what to do."

I swallow the lump in my throat and blink to clear the tears from my eyes. I've never felt so far from knowing what to do.

"I'm glad you're home," he says.

"I'm glad you're home too."

"I know this isn't what you had in mind." He states this evenly, a fact.

I shrug. "It's not what any of us had in mind. But that's okay. I wouldn't be anywhere else."

"As happy as I am to have you home, we both know this isn't where you belong," he says. "When all is said and done, I hope you know you don't have to stay here."

"As soon as the coast is clear, I'm out of here," I say. "I'm thinking Paris."

He chuckles. "Good. Let me know when I can visit."

I nod. We both know there will be no Paris.

We fall into silence, glancing again around the room. 20 years after we spent most afternoons playing card games on the floor, our lives have crashed back together and once again we inhabit this space together. We've both left and come back to the place where so many things began, and where, both of us realize as we sit together in the silence of late afternoon, so many will end.

On afternoons that feel normal, when Dad is napping or watching television and Mom is cleaning or rearranging more drawers, I take a break from job and apartment hunting and drive Dad's van around Kalamazoo, making wrong turns and doubling back, wasting time and gas, lost and then found and then lost again. I pass by the diner on Stadium Drive and remember drinking bottomless cups of sludgy coffee and laughing until curfew. I drive by Sweetwater's Donut Mill where I spent my first gainfully employed summer serving up coffee and over 30 kinds of donuts. I drive down Gull Road toward Richland, out past the farms, toward my ex-boyfriend's house. For a minute I think he's there playing kickball with the dog in the front yard, waiting for me. But that was 12 years ago. The passage of time stuns me, leaves me feeling guilty and invisible and utterly misplaced. As I speed down the road in a futile attempt to outrun time and death, it seems that my attempts to right myself will only make things worse, like a lost hiker who unwittingly goes deeper and deeper into the woods.

* * *

Visiting landmarks of my teenage years brings me one day to Vicksburg, where I drive around looking for a reservation off U Avenue. I used to go there with a kid I'd met at the donut mill who had a fondness for the grounds because it was legal to hunt in some areas; we'd hear rifle shots echo in the background every now and then and he'd crash suddenly to the ground as if under fire, grinning.

It's a beautiful day, so I decide to walk around the reservation and try to enjoy it. Maybe I'm not paying attention to where I'm going, or maybe the layout of the reservation has changed; within 15 minutes I'm picking through brambles, thinking that I'm looping back toward the car, but then encountering a marshy stretch I've never seen before. My feet slide into the ground and my laces come untied, pulled loose by the thick muck. The harder I try to move, the worse it is, and twice I sink up to my calves. I grab at branches to pull myself back up; the branches are full of thorns. I talk to myself, first in my mind and then out loud: *I hate this, I hate this, I hate this*. I hate this beautiful trip to the beautiful woods.

Something snaps. I become furious. *Fuck, fuck, fuck*, says my voice. *Just get me to my car and let me go home*, I scream inside my head to no one, to the world. I want to hose off my feet, throw my shoes in the washing machine, put peroxide on my arms. But I can't get through the woods, can't find the trail I've somehow lost. I'm tempted to stop and have a proper tantrum, but my desperation to get back to the car propels me through thick patches of bush and bramble. Sweat coats my entire body, stinging my eyes and dripping down my face, but I don't wipe it away, don't wipe away anything. Leaves and twigs poke through my tank top, vines curl and snag at my waist, gnats stick to the sweat on my chest. Spider webs and dirt and burrs press against me as if to say, this is the world growing thick in front of your face, sharp and feisty as hell. Even if you get through this part, soon enough you'll find yourself with a face full of thorns again.

Eventually the sound of traffic seeps into the edges of my consciousness and I follow it to the road, which leads me to my car. As I settle into the driver's seat, I get a look at myself in the mirror. My face, neck, shoulders, and arms are blazing and puffy, lined with dirt and dried blood. The scratches stand bright and angry against my sad, pale skin.

The face in the mirror is nearly unrecognizable in its defiance of injury, the hard-set eyes and clenched jaw, nostrils flaring. For a minute I'm shocked blank of all thought. Careful to avoid looking at myself in the rearview mirror, I turn the key in the ignition and disappear into traffic.

On the way home, I see the tall and gleaming sign of the new supermarket. Impulsively, I turn into the parking lot. I pick the sticks out of my hair and dump the water from my water bottle over my shoes to rinse off some of the muck. I wipe my muddy feet at the door and stroll purposefully into the store.

The supermarket is a recurring location in *White Noise*. All those people pushing carts, contemplating, trying to right the squeaky wheel that keeps veering left, buying things they think will keep them alive. All those people I think are nothing like me until we shuffle together under the bright white lights, cheek-bones sinking, chests caving.

"The men consult lists, the women do not. There is a sense of wandering now, an aimless and haunted mood, sweet-tempered people taken to the edge. They scrutinize the small print on packages, wary of a second level of betrayal. The men scan for stamped dates, the women for ingredients. Many have trouble making out the words. Smeared print, ghost images. In the altered shelves, the ambient roar, in the plain and heartless fact of their decline, they try to work their way through confusion. But in the end it doesn't matter what they see or think they see. The terminals are equipped with holographic scanners, which decode the binary secret of every item, infallibly. This is the language of waves and radiation, or how the dead speak to the living. And this is where we wait together, regardless of age, our carts stocked with brightly colored goods. A slowly moving line, satisfying, giving us time to glance at the tabloids in the racks. The tales of the supernatural and the extraterrestrial. The miracle vitamins, the cures for cancer, the remedies for obesity. The cults of the famous and the dead."

My shoes squelch and seep water as I wander aimlessly down the aisles looking for foods that are gentle and bland, neither too hot nor too cold. There's a Starbucks in the store. Seedless watermelons are on sale. I press honeydew between my hands, pretending I know how to test its ripeness. Lobsters scrabble around a big tank, their eyes bulging like pinheads. The choices of rice overwhelm me—I pick the kind in the plastic container, the one that could survive a fall.

A trail of wet and muddy footprints marks my zigzag trail across the store. Other shoppers watch me—I can feel their glances flitting around me like flies. It occurs to me that I might see someone I know, but I can't find the energy to care. I take both instant and stovetop pudding, chocolate, vanilla, and strawberry. I buy some Ensure, Ginger Ale, soft dinner rolls, Saltines. If someone looked into my cart they would think I had a sick child at home.

I stand in front of the Shiraz, shifting my weight from one foot to another. I drift toward the Malbecs and Cabernets. As I scan the labels, I taste the tannins on my tongue and my stomach turns. I do something I haven't done since I got violently sick off cheap white wine during my study abroad in Ireland almost ten years ago—I slide past the Rieslings and play with the neck of a bottle of Pinot Gris. With sudden force, the surprise Dad would feel if he could see me right now asserts itself—he knows I don't like white wine. This seals it; I put the bottle in my cart. I drink white now. Things have changed.

I pay with a credit card, a challenge for the slow

cashier. My feet ooze mud onto the floor as I fish my wallet back out of my pocket to get my card for her to run through again, and then a third time. The transaction completes and I shamble out, paper sacks clutched to my chest, leaving footprints all the way to the car.

* * *

I lie sleepless in my old bed, peering through the dark at the outlines of Dad's things on the desk. How many nights have I lain here, sleepless over a feverish crush or anxious about a test, my eyes sweeping the room, resting in corners, searching for dark spots on the walls that might be spiders? How many nights I've either been lulled to sleep or yanked from it by snoring from the other side of the wall. Tonight the only noise I hear is the whirring of the oxygen machine, dutifully recycling and dispensing air.

In my head, the word "Dad" echoes over and over, a syllable on an endless loop. A feeling of panic rises in my chest, a frantic rush that, after its initial shock, registers as familiar. I shut my eyes and remember lying in bed, always a light sleeper, waking to the sound of Dad's soft footsteps at four in the morning in anticipation of an early tee time. I must have been seven or eight the first time, and then it became a ritual that continued all through high school, usually on Sunday mornings. Rigid, blankets pulled up to my chin as though any movement might give away my trespass into consciousness, I'd listen as he walked down the hall, flicked a lightswitch and closed the bathroom door. I'd hear a flush, running water, the scrub of a toothbrush. A few minutes later, the refrigerator opened, a glass of orange juice clinked softly on the counter. My heart pounded as he shook his keys into his pocket and pulled a jacket from the closet. When he opened the front door, I'd be seized by the nearly combustible urge to burst out the front door after him and fling myself around one of his sturdy legs. Maybe I wanted to stop him from driving off. Or maybe I just wanted him to know that while the rest of the world was still sleeping, I was up too. That he wouldn't have to meet the rising dawn alone.

Making Luck

"Luck arranged things so that a baby named Malachi Constant was born the richest child on Earth. On the same day, luck arranged things so that a blind grandmother stepped on a roller skate at the head of a flight of cement stairs, a policeman's horse stepped on an organ grinder's monkey, and a paroled bank robber found a postage stamp worth nine hundred dollars in the bottom of a trunk in his attic."

Kurt Vonnegut, *Sirens of Titan*

Three days after I moved to New York City, ready to conquer adulthood and more confident than ever that I was truly the ruler of my own destiny, the sound of an airplane flying into the World Trade Center woke me up. I turned on the television and, for a while, forgot I was actually there, that this was happening outside my door. I didn't know which way the avenues ran or where to go when bad things happened. I didn't know anyone except for my cat, who ventured out from wherever she'd been hiding from the city noise, sniffing the new silence.

From my roof I watched traffic backing up across

bridges, towers smoking like unfiltered cigarettes, the stunned and stilted peeling away from the carnage. After the first tower fell, I decided to head north. A cab already carrying four passengers stopped for me. They all knew people who might be dead; they all also had families and friends to be with. I haunted the line between lucky and unlucky.

During the next dusty stretch of days, I walked the eerily empty streets wearing a surgical mask pressed into my hand by a Red Cross volunteer, watched by the hundreds of faces on missing posters. Everyone was exceedingly polite—there was no honking at busy intersections, no birds being flipped, no expletives. Most of us were shell-shocked, but staying numb took work. The bars were packed; when we were drunk, everything made equally little sense.

The economic repercussions of September 11 landed like a suckerpunch—we all saw it coming just in time to realize there was no avoiding it. Hiring freezes and layoffs swept the city. The nonprofit organization I was supposed to work for withdrew their offer. My bank account hemorrhaged. The owner of the apartment I was subletting sold the building, and I needed a new place to live.

A few days after 9/11, I sat on my bedroom floor, overwhelmed by the mess around me. If you've ever put off cleaning your room for months, you know what this is like. You look around, disaster everywhere, and can't figure out how or where to start. I called my best friend, Mark, for consolation.

What he said was, "well, we do make our own luck."

As the words registered, I felt accused and insulted and shamed. What could I possibly have done to cause the apartment problem, the job retraction, the flying of planes into buildings? He wasn't blaming me for September 11, but he was suggesting that I fit into it somehow, or that it fit into me. I argued that I had no control over the events happening around me. Yet what he said disconcerted me; it presupposed that I was a powerful force—an unbelievable and terrifying proposition. And I had to wonder: if we make our own luck, what does that say about the people who were on the airplanes or trapped in the towers?

This is the same question I ask myself whenever something horrible happens to someone, especially someone I know. Especially me.

* * *

I had no job and no friends, which left too much time to think, and transformed 9/11 into a diving board for endless ruminations. This tragedy wasn't about my personal philosophies or attempts to square myself with the ways of the world, but I didn't know what else to do with it. By the time it occurred to me to donate blood, all the blood banks in the city were full. Mayor Giuliani told residents that there were too many volunteers at Ground Zero and asked us to check back in a couple weeks. Even when I wandered the streets, my mind moved more than my feet. I couldn't clean up the mess and I couldn't stop thinking about what it all meant.

When marathon sessions in front of the television grew overwhelming and tiresome, I moved to the bookshelf to seek comfort in the familiar wear of spines and the smell of old paper. Certain books had morphed in meaning in the past week, such as *Skinny Legs and All*, *White Noise*, and most of my science fiction; the cover of *Underworld* had become uncanny and foreboding. In my head, I posed questions to my library as though consulting an oracle. My thumb grazed the purple cover of Kurt Vonnegut's *Sirens of Titan* and stopped. The idea that the foibles of luck render obsessing about one's purpose in life a waste of time and energy resonated deeply. A couple hundred pages in, the protagonist, Malachi Constant, finally realizes that he has no control over the trajectory of his life:

"'What happened to you?' said the congregation…

'I was a victim of a series of accidents, as are we all,' he said.

The cheering and dancing began again."

As I skimmed through, Vonnegut seemed to pat my knee and tell me that nothing was my fault. Like Malachi Constant, my present circumstance was created by a series of accidents, dice rolls, short straws. Bad luck. Initially, I found the idea comforting—what was Mark's flippant psychobabble next to the infinite wisdom of Kurt Vonnegut?

If luck is the force that moves the world, not everything is about me, or you, or anyone—perhaps not much is. As I stood, my hand pressed to the book as though it were a Bible, I realized that accepting my luck, or the sheer arbitrariness of my situation, was tantamount to admitting that there was nothing I could do, now or ever. While there's a certain comfort in powerlessness and in the idea that all we can do is keep going, I found it problematically passive.

If we embrace blind luck, we cede our agency and disconnect ourselves from cause and effect. Luck removes us from personal fault and responsibility, but it feels like an empty explanation, a cop out. 9/11 was a consequence of years of logistical planning, as well as hatred toward the U.S. and its policies. The towers fell because planes flew into them; that part wasn't luck. The haziness comes in when I consider the people involved in 9/11 through no choice of their own—the people on the planes, in the towers, on the sidewalk. Even people like me, outsiders suddenly thrust into a crumbling labyrinth to discover that the path people had used to find their way before didn't exist anymore. All of us who felt disoriented, like we'd been strapped half-conscious into a seat on the Tilt-A-Whirl, unable to get off.

In *Sirens of Titan*, Malachi Constant fumbles his way through a life that, unbeknownst to him, has been laid out. He commits the folly of believing in his own agency, and then we simultaneously wince and laugh as we realize that he's a pawn in a ridiculously specific and poignantly absurd grand scheme. Vonnegut chides us for becoming so consumed with the search for meaning that our purpose in life becomes finding out our purpose in life. However, Vonnegut was a humanist, which means that he believed in people's ability to learn, to change, and to determine the course of their lives. He didn't believe that life is just a series of accidents, and neither do I.

The tricky part is that just when I think I've got some part of this figured out, something else happens to make me reconsider. A few years later, when my Dad was diagnosed with stage-four cancer, I wasn't so sure. Mark's words haunted me again, this time taking on an even more personal heft than they had before. My dad hadn't made this luck for himself, had he? He was relatively young, strong, and healthy; he exercised, drank only occasionally, didn't smoke, lacked a genetic disposition for cancer, and had hardly been sick a day in his life. What's more, he was engaged with life, excited and stimulated by his job teaching political science, and by his various hobbies, including golfing, swimming, and collecting buttons. In my mind, he lived exactly the way people *should* live. So what insidious force in the world was to blame for his cancer, and for his death? Or was it simply an accident, a turn of bad luck? And from which of these two possibilities could I glean any understanding or solace?

Buddhists believe that nothing is an accident; that luck (or lack thereof), skills, and even the way someone looks are all results of past actions. What we've done in our previous lives determines the qualities, including luck itself, we possess in our current lives. If something appears to happen by chance, it's because we don't yet understand the relationship. We can make or change our luck over the course of a few lifetimes, but we're born into our current lives with a finite amount of luck.

The idea of luck being finite raises all sorts of questions. Can we stockpile it by staying away from Vegas and the stock market? Can we use it all up in one glorious burst, or is it meted out? Since luck exists in both quantity and quality, do some people get a heap of better-than-average luck and others a dash of extraordinary luck? 9/11 generated stories of near-misses, people whose alarms failed to go off that morning, thus saving their lives, or the secretary who had just stepped out to make a bagel run. How much luck did these people use by surviving that day? Did the people who didn't survive simply run out of luck?

In the Hindu system of karma, one can actually earn luck, so presumably one needn't run out. Karma also connects luck to cause and effect; beneficial events result from past beneficial actions and harmful events from past harmful actions. Karma accumulates and returns, sometimes unexpectedly, years or decades later, or in one's next life. Good actions build good karma, which generates good luck, suggesting that good luck can be earned and is linked to what one deserves.

Any system that guides us toward earning luck is incompatible with the idea that luck is random, which is especially confusing in the context of 9/11. After Dad's diagnosis, I would sift through these incompatibilities again and again. As much as I want to believe in a universal system of fairness, under which we ultimately get what we deserve, I would rather believe that bad luck causes bad things happen to good people than to believe that good people did something along the way to deserve what they got.

Sometimes, I feel I've earned good luck when I've suffered a run of bad. This line of thought isn't really about earning anything—it's about the law of averages, the assertion that luck functions like the economy, that a boom follows a depression. During hard times, we can console ourselves with the belief that our luck is bound to change. This also means that good fortune won't or can't go unchallenged for long, so we can either appreciate our good luck while it lasts or wait for the other shoe to drop. Next to the complexities of luck and karma, the tendency toward the mean provides a practical and mathematical explanation for luck's vicissitudes. Then again, as Vonnegut says, "some people are lucky and other people aren't and not even a graduate of Harvard Business School can say why."

On September 11, 26-year-old Hilda Yolanda Mayol, an employee at a restaurant on the ground floor of the World Trade Center, escaped before the building collapsed. Two months later, American Airlines Flight 587 crashed into a neighborhood in Queens, killing all 260 passengers, including Hilda Yolanda Mayol, who was on her way to the Dominican Republic for a vacation. As dissatisfying as the explanation might be, I prefer thinking that Hilda was a victim of a series of accidents, an unfortunate recipient of a big dose of bad luck, rather than thinking that she earned this outcome. I feel the same way about my dad. However, unlike my dad's situation, Hilda's luck doesn't appear random—though of course it could be a coincidence that she was involved in both tragedies, it's hard to avoiding concluding that her luck seemed geared toward a specific outcome, namely, her untimely death. If luck has an agenda, I'm even more wary of its role in shaping our lives.

Before I moved to New York, I travelled to Morocco. Within a single city such as Fez or Marrakesh, there's an old city and a new city. The new city has McDonald's, alcohol, and women in short skirts, whereas the old city, the Medina, has no electricity or running water. The clay walls of the alleyways are covered with sticks that distill sunlight into the grey of in-betweens, the color of the donkeys that walk by. Kids work at the tannery, pressing skins with their bare feet while they rub their swollen bellies. School is a room carved out of large rock where students sit on the ground and strain to read stone tablets.

I've never felt so lucky and humbled simply to have been born to my parents in Michigan, to be who I am. These kids weren't so lucky. Neither were the Berbers on the trains who had to handcuff baskets of marketplace goods to their wrists, afraid that someone might steal them should they fall asleep. Had they done something in a previous life to warrant being born into their circumstances or was it luck? I wonder how much luck I've used up just being me. I wonder how it is decided who gets to be born in Kalamazoo, Michigan, and who will be born in the Medina where the donkeys and the people drink from the same trough.

Perhaps it's reductive, but I can't shake the notion that someone's behind the curtain. Luck, even if random, is a force with energy and movement. It has to come from somewhere—every force has a genesis. Is luck born like a thunderclap when certain conditions exist? What or who is luck? Karma raises the same question—if karma is a reaction, who or what is reacting? Who or what determines the poetic justice that will extend over multiple lifetimes? Karma is a system, which suggests that it needs to be managed.

Luck seems to be a system too, though I can't discern what rules or ruler governs it. If luck operates on a scale or system, why can't the outcomes be programmed or predicted?

If nothing else, luck is thick with idiosyncrasies; when luck sticks its finger in the pot and stirs things up, it evades understanding. Chewing over luck's inner-workings is like running in a hamster wheel. Even if we can't make sense of luck, we can make sense of the choices we make in its wake, which brings me back to Mark's comment and our power to change things.

The idea that I can release energy into the world that will somehow come back to me seems naive, even hokey. Sometimes I think the world is too complicated for an idea like that. Other times, I think it's so simple and obvious that it must be true; perhaps impossibility is more perception than physics. Of course a person's outlook can change things, but can it actually make luck? It's egocentric to believe that the ripples spreading from my choices can actually change the world. Except, isn't that what we're supposed to believe? The power of one person—each of us—to change the world?

We have the power to transform our surroundings, whether it's by leveling a rainforest, building a house, or planting flowers. Given my transience, I wasn't sure how to use this power beyond packing and unpacking.

Then I met Liz. Her apartment wasn't any bigger or nicer than anyone else's, but you'd walk inside and feel comfortable, lighter, like you're breathing different air. I asked her how she did it and she introduced me to feng shui, an ancient Chinese system of environmental arrangement by which the intentional placement of objects produces energy that changes one's life. Initially, I was skeptical. Feng shui seemed like reason to go overboard with Oriental furnishings—Liz had dragons, coins, bamboo, water foundations, and crepe lanterns. Still, it wasn't what she had—it was how everything was arranged. Harmonious placement, or the successful practice of feng shui, makes spaces *feel* good.

Feng shui is an easy and risk-free way to try and change one's life, and it's fun to move furniture around like an interactive puzzle until the pieces click. The guidelines of feng shui involve being clear in your intentions when placing objects. It makes sense that where we put our stuff affects the energy of a space— if we're haphazard about the objects that surround us, we surrender control of our environment. September 11 proved how little environmental control we sometimes have, but when it comes to our personal space, we don't have to surrender that control. "You wouldn't let someone else dress you every day, would you?" Liz asked.

The proof that feng shui works isn't a specific outcome. If you rearrange the furniture or change the lighting you're already realizing your control over your environment. It works because you're *moving*, which is the only way to change. Even just swapping the coffee table and the couch can help people recapture a feeling of agency and believe in the possibility of other changes. Of course, all the feng shui in the world couldn't cure Dad's cancer, but it would be silly to think that it could. What it did do was to alleviate, at least a little bit, that pervasive feeling of impotence one has when she can't fix something or someone. While engaged in moving objects in the health area of my parents' home, I felt some amount of control, even if it was only temporary. Maybe he was humoring me, but my dad seemed to feel it too as he helped me pick out a new plant for that part of the house, a new mobile to hang, a new color to introduce. We were both engaged in the task of changing our environment, which at least for one afternoon, made us both feel that we were doing something to make the situation better.

Practicing feng shui, especially after 9/11, may be the closest I've come to making luck. A few weeks after I carefully set up the career area of my bedroom, I found a job as a paralegal. My cat and I moved into a nicer apartment. My life began to feel manageable. Then, during the second night at the new apartment, one of my roommates left the patio window open and in the morning, my cat was gone. The patio led, through a series of narrow openings and curled fencing, to the roof of an adjacent house, then to another, and another. I walked these rooftops, but Zola was nowhere to be found. I waited, hoping she was just hiding, anxious about the new apartment, but by the third day it was clear she was missing. My cat, who had been my constant and sometimes only companion since college, and who had never before been outdoors, was somewhere out there on the mean streets of Manhattan, lost.

I risked my new job by calling in sick. I plastered flyers around the neighborhood and walked streets calling her name. I felt as though the world had collapsed. My cat was gone and my life—and, it seemed, the very future of the universe—hung in the balance. Karma or chance or luck could take jobs and apartment buildings, but taking my cat, especially after all that had happened, was hitting below the belt.

I took another day off work. I sat on the floor with my legs tucked under me, feeling like a lost five-year-old. My tiny room stuffed with moving boxes suddenly seemed huge, a space I could never inhabit no matter how much unpacking or rearranging I did. The world, which a couple of weeks earlier had wobbled precariously, had simply stopped making sense. I didn't understand the way it worked, but I knew I didn't want to be in a world that worked this way.

Again, I found myself wandering the streets, this time in search of something specific. When I wasn't looking for Zola, my thoughts once again tangled like yarn and found their way back to Vonnegut, whose life demonstrates how the world works, or doesn't. In 1944, on Mother's Day, his mother committed suicide. Later that year, the Germans captured Vonnegut during the Battle of the Bulge. When the Allied forces firebombed Dresden, Vonnegut was one of seven American POWs who survived; in what seems to be a stroke of bizarre luck, he happened to be working in an underground meat locker at the time of the attack.

Vonnegut smoked unfiltered Pall Mall cigarettes from the age of 12 and joked about suing Pall Mall's manufacturer: "I'm eighty-three years old. The lying bastards! On the package Brown & Williamson promised to kill me. Their cigarettes didn't work." In 1984, Vonnegut tried to kill himself with pills and alcohol. In 2000, he was in bed watching the Super Bowl when his ashtray overturned and started a fire. He didn't die until 2007.

Vonnegut's life exemplifies luck at its most confusing and complex. He tried to die and he couldn't, thereby turning luck on its head—unlucky to live and lucky to die. Then again, if he hadn't lived through so much, he wouldn't have written *Sirens of Titan* or *Slaughterhouse Five*. He wrote *Sirens of Titan* as satire because the innerworkings of life are ridiculous, and our attempts to force them into order only make them more ridiculous. However, Vonnegut does believe in choice—we can choose to be victims, or to smoke three packs a day, or to laugh in the face of life's oddities. We can choose to believe in luck, karma, coincidence, or God. We can choose to believe in our ability to react and to change the world, however much or however little.

I tried to stop grasping at cosmic explanations for the events of that sunny Tuesday morning and for all that followed. While losing Zola was, ironically, even more personally devastating than 9/11, it provided a smaller problem to solve. If I couldn't do anything about 9/11 and its many implications, I *had* to find the cat. There was simply no alternative, especially if I wanted to restore some sense of balance in my life.

On my third day off work, in the backyard of a Nigerian art gallery about a block away, I found Zola crouched, literally scared stiff, behind a woodpile. Back at my apartment, I watched her slowly realize that, somehow, she was home. Saved. The world regained a recognizable shape. That is, until the next time something turned my world upside down, which I'm learning never stops happening. What does change, though, is the meaning we glean from these experiences—or rather, the meaning we give these experiences.

I knew just how improbable it was that I found Zola. Cosmically, I'm not sure I understand why I found her, just as I didn't understand why I'd lost her in the first place. How much was luck and how much was me? Perhaps it didn't matter—at least for the moment, the world spun a bit straighter on its axis and I stood straighter on mine. The mess was still there, but it didn't seem so bad anymore. Just as the cranes downtown moved metal girders one by one, I picked up a piece—at first, it was as small and simple as a sock—and started moving. For the first time, I understood why people sing when they clean.

Letters to Ray Bradbury

Dear Ray Bradbury:

You are my hero.

The only other person I've ever said that to is my dad.

Dear Ray Bradbury:

I've wanted to write you a letter for a long time. I'm a teacher and I almost had my class write you letters when we were reading *The Martian Chronicles*. There are a few Douglas Spauldings in my class. A couple Clarices. They'd have talked your ear off. The furious scratch of their pencils would have left little holes in the paper.

Most of them would have expressed admiration for your prophetic insights about the paranoias, preoccupations, and prejudices of society. You've blown their minds with your prescience about trigger-happiness, the addiction of colonization, xenophobia, cultural intolerance, laziness, loneliness, our increasing tendency to invent our own realities when we want something badly enough, and the fact that we'd sell hotdogs on Mars if there were money in it.

My kids are too young to understand this, but somehow they do, and they would have written to you about it: you have your finger on the dark pulse of humanity, yet you spend far more time exploring and being fascinated by it than you do chastising or worrying. You see the ugliness, but you still believe in and love people. This means we can believe you. You're not here to fool us—you're here to open us up. We all want to know what you know, what gives you insight and optimism at the same time, so we'll go wherever you take us.

They'd have asked you questions. What do you think about Pluto getting demoted? Have you ever been visited by aliens? How might America implement the happy triangle of art, science, and religion that you imagine on Mars? Do you believe in time travel? Do you believe in God?

One or two of them would have described to you in detail their new tennis shoes. They would have wriggled their toes and wished they could run and write at the same time.

Maybe I'm projecting. Maybe I'm thinking about what I would have said if I'd written you a letter.

March 12, 2007

Dear Ray Bradbury:

My students, who are twelve to fourteen years old, read *The Martian Chronicles* a few weeks ago. What a joy it was, in the dreary Michigan February, to pull out this book and give them the best kind of homework.

I had them define science fiction. Then I promised them their definitions would change after they read your book.

"Whoa!" they all said.

"This book is not what I expected," they said.

"It's about people!"

They debated Spender's guilt with all the seriousness of greenhorn lawyers. In an attempt to explain the encounter in "Night Meeting," they invented theories of how time works on Mars. They created Martian masks, wore them, and became powerful. They mourned the realization that one of the few qualities that separate humans from animals or other sentient races is our use of guns. "Usher II" drove them mad with delight; one student said that the "Investigator of Moral Climates" made him think of our administration ruling by "red tape and fear." My heart and mind constantly turned cartwheels when we talked about your book.

We examined the Martian purpose of life. "Why live? Life was its own answer. Life was the propagation of more life and the living of as good a life as possible. Life was now good and needed no arguments."

"This thing is good," became a class catch phrase.

We marveled at your writing ("I'm learning so much new vocabulary! 'Rococo' is totally my new favorite word!"), your imagination, your vision. When we got to "There Will Come Soft Rains," one shiny-eyed student raised her hand and said, "That house was more human than any other character in the book." They got that beautiful hurt in them when the house died. And they loved it.

This is how I know my students have souls.

This is why I wanted to write you a letter.

March 17, 2007

Dear Ray Bradbury:

I taught synesthesia to my students today. I tied it in with *The Martian Chronicles'* themes about aesthetics and psychic evolution. I brought in Ken Croswell's book on Mars, with mind-blowing high-definition photographs that give palpable texture to Mars' surface; ice floes look like designs drawn in mercury, clouds are crowds of bubbles. One could read those pictures like Braille.

In the book there's a close-up of Phobos orbiting Mars. Phobos looks like a dumpling with its side pinched down, like a knobby fist. I can't look at it without getting a lump in my throat—it is the most forlorn thing I've ever seen. It reminds me of a line from *The Martian Chronicles*—how Earth looks like a "lonely baseball" from outer space.

I brought in some IDM (intelligent dance music) and ambient sounds—Autechre, Aphex Twin, Boards of Canada—you know, the stuff associated either implicitly or explicitly with alien landscapes. They listened to the music and paged through the book, tracing the shapes, sensations moving from ears to fingers to eyes to mind. They drew and wrote about how they thought Mars would look and smell and feel.

For long stretches of time they sat with their eyes shut, listening to the music. "This song is so…purple," someone would say.

"Yeah!" someone else would say. "I hear purple too."

"This song feels like one of those stress balls that you can smoosh in your hand."

"I smell fireworks!"

"This thing is good," someone said.

We all agreed that our class on synesthesia was, per your book, a "Martian" experience. The ability to mix senses and sensory experiences is one of the ways the Martians in your book are more evolved than the humans. Someone said that next time, we should invite you. What do you say, Mr. Bradbury? Would you like to hang out with my class and draw music?

March 26, 2007

Dear Ray Bradbury:

My students recently read an essay called "How the Lawyers Stole Winter," by Christopher Daly. The piece is about how much times have changed, especially for kids. Daly reminisces about skating on a pond as a kid and bemoans the fact that kids nowadays aren't allowed to—there are fences, danger signs and parents too scared to let their kids outside, much less onto a frozen lake.

My students talked about how none of them play outside very much. The times when all the neighbor kids congregated on someone's lawn for a game of hide-and-go-seek are over. It's dangerous out there, so the parents keep their children in, which only makes it more dangerous.

They talked about the amount of time they, their families and their friends spend online, playing video games, and watching television. No one's going to fall through the ice doing that.

They all have cell phones.

Childhood is so different now than it was fifty, thirty or just ten years ago. It seems as though the Douglas Spaulding moments are fewer and farther between.

"It's not as innocent as it was," one of my students said.

"It's not as innocent as it should be," said another.

I asked if any of them had ever had an invisible friend. Two of them raised their hands. We talked about what that meant. One of the girls in the front stared at me, eyes wide. "Oh my gosh," she said. "It *is* the death of imagination. Almost anything we could've imagined is online or in a video game, so most people don't bother. What would happen if everyone stopped imagining?"

They were silent. Perhaps a little worried, and probably vowing to themselves that their imaginations would never die. They seemed to be experiencing nostalgia for the childhood they should have had.

"This thing isn't good," someone said.

I looked at their round open faces. They looked innocent, like babes. The idea that they weren't—that they couldn't be—was unspeakably sad for all of us.

"Can we read something uplifting?" one of them asked.

Lucky for them I had just the thing. Before class I'd run copies of "On the Shoulders of Giants." There's nothing like a Bradbury essay to cure the blues:

"Comes the Evolution. The survival of that species called Child. The children, dying of starvation, hungry for ideas which lay all about in this fabulous land, locked into machines and architecture, struck out on their own. What did they do?

They walked into classrooms in Waukesha and Peoria and Neepawa and Cheyenne and Moose Jaw and Redwood City and placed a gentle bomb on a teacher's desk. Instead of an apple it was Asimov.

'What's that?' the teacher asked, suspiciously.

'Try it. It's good for you,' said the students.

'No thanks.'

'Try it,' said the students. 'Read the first page. If you don't like it, stop.' And the clever students turned and went away.

The teachers (and the librarians, later) put off reading, kept the book around the house for a few weeks and then, late one night, tried the first paragraph.

And the bomb exploded.

They not only read the first but the second paragraph, the second and third pages, the fourth and fifth.

'My God!' they cried, almost in unison, 'these damned books are *about* something!'"

My students cheered for children. Their renewed faith in imagination—in themselves—ran through them, flushing their cheeks.

Their next set of papers was all magic thunder. They invented alien races (one of which worshipped duct tape), they wrote about six-headed dragons, their characters spoke in devilish riddles, and their poems morphed into blank-verse epics.

Covering those papers with exclamation points, checkmarks, and smiley faces wasn't enough. I should have put those papers in a time capsule and buried it in my backyard. Dug it up two years later, five, ten—whenever we needed it. I'd unearth it one day and read the stories and we would learn this lesson again, in case we'd forgotten. Or even if we hadn't.

April 2, 2007

Dear Ray Bradbury:

I read *Zen in the Art of Writing* on a bus to Copenhagen. It was a used copy—the pages were slightly worn and the corners were a little greasy. They had creases like wrinkles on a face.

Two thirds of the way through the preface, my heart broke. I cried as though a dam had burst behind my eyes. I didn't care who saw me; I was on a bus ten thousand miles away from anyone or anything I knew. I cried for all it was worth.

I should probably explain.

It wasn't just that I was reading your book—it was that I was reading it at that precise moment, under those exact circumstances. My fairy godmother might've put that book into my hands.

The exact circumstances were these: my dad was dead.

We were supposed to go to Sweden together—we'd talked about the trip for ages. Now, I had in my bag a glass jar filled with his ashes. The last day of my trip I would spread them over Hedemora, where my grandfather's grandparents had lived. I got up every morning and had to figure out how I would say goodbye that day. Each footfall was a goodbye. Every blink, every yawn, every drop of rain.

I travelled alone. He was the only person who belonged with me on that trip. Most days I was socked by the one-two-three of awe, sadness, and anger. I'd see something beautiful and seconds later the awe transformed to sadness that he couldn't see it. Then I'd get mad, because he should've been there.

I got caught in the hamster wheel, spinning around and around the fact that It Wasn't Fair. No matter how many times I ran around it, no matter how many angles from which I examined it, that fact never changed. At least when I travelled, I was actually going somewhere instead of pacing around my apartment. Working that fact through my body instead of around it, getting it out of my system.

I tried to be Martian about it. As long as there was awe, I would be okay. I was halfway around the world; I could give up the habit of compartmentalizing. I could let myself feel all three emotions at once, distinctly, despite the discomfort. And maybe then I could grok things more fully.

Exposition is never easy, is it?

April 6, 2007

Dear Ray Bradbury:

Your book is a guide to writing, but on the bus to Copenhagen, it became a guide to living.

I missed my dad all the time, completely and loudly. When I was submerged in grief, I felt more like myself than I had since he died. Being his daughter was the most stable identity I had. Yet I kept thinking to myself, how can this person who's got her father's ashes in her bag possibly be me?

During those moments I didn't know myself as anything other than a girl who had lost her dad and was desperately trying to find him again. No other parts of me existed.

After a while, though, other parts of me peeked out. We're still here, they'd say. Underneath all this.

You'll see us soon.

Zen in the Art of Writing made the writer part of me, who had been hiding for over a year, emerge, albeit shakily. I was thrilled to see her and gave her permission to appreciate the surges of emotion, the wash of tears during my rides on public transportation, the poignancy of me visiting the fatherland alone. The writer part of me filled notebooks. This is important, she said. This means something. I should write about this.

The daughter part of me answered, this is sacred. If you're going to write about it, write about it. Don't say you're going to write about it and then mope around the house instead.

The writer part of me got sheepish. I know, I know, it said. I won't do that. The writer in me remembered one of the last things my dad ever said to me. I told him that I would dedicate my first book to him and he said, "Thank you. But you have to finish it first."

It was during these talks between my daughter self and my writer self that I read the preface of your book.

Is it gauche to quote you to yourself? Do you think, I know all this already? Or do you think, damn, *I* wrote that. Good for me. It goes without saying that

I hope for the latter. You wrote this, and it's perfect. Hot damn:

"What, you ask, does writing teach us?

First and foremost, it reminds us that we are alive and that it is a gift and privilege, not a right. We must earn life once it has been awarded us. Life asks for rewards back because it has favored us with animation.

So while our art cannot, as we wish it could, save us from wars, privation, envy, greed, old age, or death, it can revitalize us amidst it all.

Second, writing is survival. Any art, any good work, of course, is that.

Not to write, for many of us, is to die.

We must take arms each and every day, perhaps knowing that the battle cannot be entirely won, but fight we must, if only a gentle bout. The smallest effort to win means, at the end of each day, a sort of victory. Remember the pianist who said that if he did not practice every day he would know, if he did not practice for two days, the critics would know, after three days, his audiences would know.

A variation of this is true for writers. Not that your style, whatever that is, would melt out of shape in those few days.

But what would happen is that the world would catch up with and try to sicken you. If you didn't write every day, the poisons would accumulate and you would begin to die, or act crazy, or both.

You must stay drunk on writing so reality cannot destroy you.

For writing allows just the proper recipes of truth, life, reality as you are able to eat, drink and digest without hyperventilating and flopping like a dead fish in your bed.

I have learned, on my journeys, that if I let a day go by without writing, I grow uneasy. Two days and I am in tremor. Three and I suspect lunacy. Four and I might as well be a hog, suffering the flux in a wallow. An hour's writing is tonic. I'm on my feet, running in circles, and yelling for a clean pair of spats.

Taking your pinch of arsenic every morn so you can survive to sunset. Another pinch at sunset so that you can more than survive until dawn.

The micro-arsenic-dose swallowed here prepares you not to be poisoned and destroyed up ahead.

Work in the midst of life is that dosage. To manipulate life, toss the bright colored orbs up to mix with the dark ones, blending a variation of truths. We use the grand and beautiful facts of existence in order to put up with the horrors that afflict us directly in our families and friends, or through the newspapers and TV.

The horrors are not to be denied. Who amongst us has not had a cancer-dead friend? Which family exists where some relative has not been killed or maimed by the automobile? I know of none. The list is endless and crushing if we do not creatively oppose it.

Which means writing as cure. Not completely, of course. You never get over your parents in the hospital or your best love in the grave.

I won't use the word therapy—it's too clean, too sterile. I only say when death slows others, you must leap to set up your diving board and dive head first into your typewriter.

I have come up with a new simile to describe myself lately. It can be yours.

Every morning I jump out of bed and step on a landmine. The landmine is me.

After the explosion, I spend the rest of the day putting the pieces together.

Now, it's your turn. Jump."

I read this on the bus to Copenhagen and the daughter and writer parts of me wept together.

A thousand times a day I dissolved into pieces and, with your help, a thousand times a day I attempted my own reconstruction.

April 17, 2007

Dear Ray Bradbury:

When you travel, you can't escape yourself. You think that because you're in some other place under some other sun looking at strange people and things, you won't be inside yourself. But you're more inside yourself than ever. It's the landmine. The explosion is loud. It's messy and painful. It just so happens that the stuff that lingers inside us is the most terrifying stuff there is. Your book helped me pull my insides out and gave me the courage to look at them. I didn't try to run away from myself. Even when I was in a museum or a sculpture garden I stared myself in the eye, looking at and around and through everything that I was without blinking. Not afraid, at least not of some things, anymore.

"...[O]nly by being truly sick can one regain health. Even beasts know when it is good and proper to throw up. Teach me how to be sick then, in the right time and place, so that I may again walk in the fields and with the wise and smiling dogs know enough to chew sweet grass," you say.

There were some tough times, like a four-day stint when it poured nonstop and all my stuff got soaked. I cried about being soggy and frustrated and cold and angry. I cried about being alone, about not having spoken to anyone in three days. I cried out of relief, because I had come so close to combustion from trying to be strong and responsible. I cried about my unfinished book, about everything in my life I was worried would remain unfinished. I cried about the carnage scattered in the wake of the landmine. I cried because I wanted my daddy.

When Dad first got sick, crying felt like ripping my heart out. I thought that pieces were being extracted that would never find their way back again. But after a stretch of daily cries, those moments became more peaceful. Not so wrenching. Sometimes, even beautiful. I realized that instead of being stoic or "over it," I'd rather be drenched in Oslo, cursing and nursing my wet feet, letting my tears fall, held fast in life's fist.

April 28, 2007

Dear Ray Bradbury:

The other night, I joined a science fiction writers group. I've never written science fiction in my life, but what the hell, right?

May 2, 2007

Dear Ray Bradbury:

My students are writing literary research papers now. About half of them are writing about *The Martian Chronicles*. This is the first time I've seen students actually excited about research papers. They want to dig till their hands get dirty. I get to see the fingerprints.

The student who cried when she read "There Will Come Soft Rains" came up to me the other day and said, "Please tell me you've read *Yestermorrow: Obvious Answers to Impossible Futures*." I confessed I hadn't. "Oh," she said, and clapped her hands. "You will just love it. I can't wait for you to read it!"

I bought a copy. Used. It's on my bookshelf now, stretched horizontally across the tops of your other books. I'm waiting to read it. In June I'm going to Eastern Europe for a month. Once again, I'm travelling solo. But not alone.

I'm amassing an arsenal of landmines and secret weapons, horse manure and cicadas, memories and dreams. Tools for reconstruction.

"If your boy is a poet, horse manure can only mean flowers to him," you say, which I love, even though I sometimes turn flowers into horse manure. I'm a great appreciator of terrible beauty, but I can get stuck and wallow in the terrible part for a while before I remember to open my eyes. To travel is to open your eyes again, wider and rounder. To see the inside of things, like Superman. To see that indeed, life is its own answer.

A couple months ago during a visit to New York, I found myself wandering around the financial district trying to peek around tarps to get a look at the construction that consumed whole blocks. It wasn't your average makeover—this one would take a long time. Maybe forever.

The enormity of the reconstruction turned my stomach. The bulldozers looked exhausted; they've spent years pushing against the immovable. Yet, there's a lesson in the bulldozer. It doesn't look at the mess and think, this will never be fixed. It doesn't ask whether the work is worth it. The bulldozer does what it does—it keeps going. There's nothing wrong with rebuilding forever. It's an apt metaphor for life. Actually, it's not a metaphor at all.

The Progress of Souls

"The earth is rude, silent, incomprehensible at first…
Be not discouraged—keep on—
there are divine things, well envelop'd;
I swear to you there are divine things
more beautiful than words can tell."
Walt Whitman, *Song of an Open Road*

Scandinavian Air flight 626

The earth floats away, drops lazily downward, unconcerned, as the plane climbs, veers sharply to the right to sweep around Detroit and, it seems to me, struggles just a bit. I have that feeling I have every time I take off in a plane—that physics are irrelevant, that the aircraft is simply too massive to achieve flight. But, like every other time, the plane noses gamely upward and soon the land parcels itself into squares, which then reveal themselves to be small pieces in larger squares. Michigan doesn't look like a mitten from above.

The seatbelt sign switches off. The flight attendant

tells us that we can use electronics, that we've success-fully reached cruising altitude, that we're safe. This is when it starts sinking in. It's like sitting in the back of a rollercoaster and seeing the first car start over the hill; there's no going back.

I have everything a traveler should have: music, books, a blank journal, a universal adapter, a flash-light, earplugs, maps, a sleep sack, my brother's lucky tiger's eye, locks, combinations. I also have a few extras: a small picture of my dad, his old baby rattle, and a jar of his ashes, carefully wrapped in orange bandanas and tucked away in my pack. We'd always planned on making this trip together. When I get to Hedemora, Sweden, the homeland of Dad's ancestors, I will spread the ashes.

Even though I've diligently armed myself, already I feel cut adrift. *Lonely Planet Scandinavia* doesn't have a chapter on pilgrimages or walkabouts, doesn't contain advice on how to travel with your dad's ashes when you should be traveling with him.

Choosing which books to take, which ones will be best to read, is the hardest part of packing. At any moment I might desperately need one of at least ten books, some of which I've read and some of which I haven't yet, but have a feeling about. I save books for trips and turn them into companions.

I'd narrowed it down to six, but the night before I left I dreamed of locomotives. Upon awaking, I stumbled over to the bookshelf and stuffed Walt Whitman's *Leaves of Grass* into my backpack. This trip seems like a good time to reread "Song of Myself," maybe try to figure out whether there are any traces left of the person I used to be, whether there's anything to recover.

The book sits open across my legs like a Bible on the lap of a lost soul. Even when I can't concentrate on it, my fingers drift over the words as I turn page after page, creating a rhythmic rustling like wings.

At some point in the middle of the night over the dark Atlantic, I turn on the overhead light and look down at the page creased beneath my worrying hands: poem 82, "Song of an Open Road." "Henceforth I whimper no more, postpone no more," Whitman says at the beginning of his journey. "Strong and content, I travel the open road." I glance out the window, catching a glimpse of my face against the blackness of the stratosphere. I don't look content or strong. I don't know if those things are out there, but if they are, Whitman would seem to have an idea of the way.

* * *

A couple months ago, my therapist tapped her temple and said to me, "processing and healing isn't all up here." She often said things like that.

I waited for her to elaborate, but she just looked at me. She often did this, too. "Are you saying that you don't think I'm emotionally processing this?" I asked.

"You're not numb—clearly you're feeling intense grief," she said. "And when you come in here, you're open and descriptive about what you've been thinking and feeling. By the time you bring it in here, you've analyzed and accounted for how you feel and when and why, and we talk about it, which is all well and good."

"But…"

"But intellectually processing something isn't the same as emotionally processing it. You can come to terms with something in your head and still not actually feel any better or act any differently. You're taking the grief and all the other painful feelings and pushing them into your head, where you can understand and explain them, where you can better deal with them," she said, hands clasped over her crossed legs.

I was annoyed; she had a point. "I've been coming here and talking myself to exhaustion, unburdening myself each week," I said. "Why bother if the process doesn't do any good?"

She smiled that bland therapist smile that makes me want to scream. "I do believe in the process and what I'm saying now is part of it. That word 'unburden' is interesting. It makes me think of laying things down, dumping them all out, no matter what they are." She smiles, uncrosses her legs and leans forward. "Do you think you've unburdened yourself here?"

I've talked to her about realizing that the world is, indeed, a terribly unfair place, and that I hate the way it works. I've talked to her about being sad and alone and feeling like a failure back here in my hometown. That I feel as though I've just woken up from years of dreaming, suddenly catapulted into an off-kilter bizarro world that might look from afar like the old one, until you get closer and realize that everything is shifted off-balance. It doesn't feel like my life—it feels like something I've borrowed or inherited but for some reason have to keep wearing. These are things I've said. I don't know what else there is.

After a minute she continued. "You use me as a sounding board, which is great, but you've got other sounding boards. More importantly, you've never laid out anything ugly in here. You've never made a mess. You've never cried." She pauses, lets it sink in. "You keep it together in here like you keep it together out there. If you can't let it go in here, where are you going to do it?"

It's true. There is so much ugliness in me that I can't let even her see it. "Okay," I said. "What should I do?"

"The answer's different for everyone," she said. "But I think you need to get out of your head. And, probably, out of this room. Take a dance class, learn a new sport, push yourself out of your comfort zone."

When I walked into session the next week, I pulled out of my purse a plane ticket to Sweden. "Something like this?" I asked. One passenger, open-ended return.

* * *

I suddenly feel very precarious, reeling near the edge of the world, conspicuously alone. I don't fear for my safety in Scandinavia, but there are always tricky logistics, inscrutable maps and timetables, language barriers, unforeseen complications. And I'm a little unsure about navigating in the shape I'm in, afraid I might fall apart as I move around with my elephantine grief and the reality of what my life is now.

I imagine what's tied up in the bandana dangling on the end of my soul's hobo stick. I carry my devastation, my grief, the high tide of mourning. I carry the knowledge of what death can do. I carry the desperate conviction that I don't want anyone to feel like this, ever. I carry the certainty that we all will anyway. I carry what's left intact, tucked inside my own penumbra, still hiding but shyly considering cultivation into something strong and true and human.

Stockholm, Sweden

Dad would love Stockholm; the aesthetic and the attitude would suit him perfectly. This city is pristine, from the precisely cut lines of its buildings to the cleanliness of the streets to the mindset of the people. Swedes comport themselves with steadfast competence and awareness. They recycle meticulously, they don't jay-walk, their trains are unfailingly punctual, everyone is aware of the position of the sun in the now almost endlessly lit sky. This modern city of electric buses and mobile devices and sleek and sensible architecture contains within it the Gamla Stan, the old town of crooked, bricked streets, alleyways, labyrinths, gothic awnings. Södermalm, the southern district and government seat, sits at the edge of the water looking over its austere and impressive kingdom backlit by the evening sun.

I go to a statue garden on a hill and look out over the city, awestruck at the city's silhouette, the shapes of the windowpanes. I wish Dad could see this. I hold on to the railing in front of me, trying to push into the cool metal the fact that I am here and he is not. He will never stand on a hill in Stockholm, will never cruise the fjords of Norway or follow the medieval wall around Tallinn. Everything I see in this moment and in all of the moments for the rest of my life are things he will not see. My fingers tighten around the railing in front of me as though I'm fixing to throttle. The wind kicks up around my face, whipping my hair against the back of my neck. I turn into it, forcing my eyes open.

The sadness slides seamlessly into anger. He should be here, he should see this—that was the plan. I'm not supposed to be here alone. It's just one of the many wrongs in this moment, in my life, in the world. My anger surprises me—it's reared its head before, but I hadn't realized the extent of my unfamiliar and frightening rage.

I skip dinner and go to bed early. As I lie there, my thoughts seize upon how surreal all this is. No one knows me; no one even knows that I'm curled up inside this sleepsack on this sagging bunk bed. If no one knows I'm here, am I really here? Do the contents of my stomach and my heart and my brain truly exist? What's really lying in a heap upon this bed?

I eventually fall asleep, hoping that when I wake up, I'll know who these arms and legs belong to, whose face appears in the mirror. Deep down, I know that some essential part of me that turns gears has been lost, that I'm on a walkabout to find it. I know it'll take more than sleep and tears to get it back, if getting it back is even possible.

Uppsala, Sweden

The rain, falling for the third straight day, beads along the windows as the bus lumbers up to Uppsala. The umbrella I bought isn't big enough to cover my pack; each night I spread my clothes out to dry them, but my next excursion soaks them again. My soggy shoes chafe my feet, I have only a damp towel to dry myself after I shower, and my books curl in on themselves. Wandering, usually my favorite way to spend time, is reduced to furtively ducking under awnings and into coffeeshops and museums. The dampness seeps into my bones and I shiver despite the humidity and the weight on my back.

I open *Leaves of Grass* across my lap and wonder

how often Whitman found himself waterlogged on the open road. I ask myself, what would Walt do?

In "Song of an Open Road," Whitman says, "Here is a man tallied—he realizes here what he has in him." It's true. Tests of both emotional and physical fortitude present themselves so often that I do have a sense of keeping score, of sorting my marks, wondering how it's all going to add up.

The rain mutes Uppsala's pink architecture to the color of dirty candy. The bus drops us at the square in the city center. I hunch under an overhang and try to read my map as raindrops seep into the paper. This is one of those times I wish I had a travel companion to help my weary and waterlogged brain, my eyes that can't read the blurred street names or figure out which way is west.

I eventually get a bus and take it to the outskirts of town to a sprawling hostel on landscaped grounds. Everything I own is soaked, which has different ramifications now that all I have is what's on my back. I've become desperately bound to these objects as though I will lose the shape of myself without them, as though I will dissolve if they do. The only reliable pieces of me are in this bag. The things I've touched, the things I wear. The journals. The papers that prove who I am.

I lay as much as I can out on the backs of chairs and bedposts and wander into the kitchen where a group of Italians cook and watch television. I plop down on a couch and wait for a chance to join the conversation. No one even looks my direction. I'm not sure what language the television program is in, but I can't begin to understand it. I wonder, again, if I am visible.

Unsure what to do with myself, I walk. If I keep walking long enough, perhaps I will meet myself again. I walk until the water squooshes out of my shoes with each step. Aside from shop clerks and bus drivers, I haven't talked to anyone in three days. I think about what would happen if I disappeared off the streets of Uppsala, lost or kidnapped or broken-legged in a ditch somewhere. Who would know? Days would go by and at some point when I hadn't answered any emails, my mom or my brother would begin to get concerned and would eventually start trying to track me down. But even they don't always know what city I'm in on a given day, much less where I'm staying. It would be weeks before anyone could do anything. Which means I'm the only one who knows just how lost I am.

Gothenburg, Sweden

For the past 28 years, much of my identity was connected to being my dad's daughter. Whereas my patrilineage used to provide a stabilizing source of pride and a clear conception of myself, it is now a gateway to emptiness. Without my dad in the world, my identity as his daughter becomes painfully inconclusive and murky. I do not say, "I am a mess," "I am a gaping hole," or "I am lonely," but every time I meet someone who asks me about myself, that's what I'm thinking as my mouth forms other, meaningless words.

Sometimes, all I am is a person walking down the street in Sweden. Sometimes I'm thirsty or tired or lost. Sometimes the bigger context drops away and in that moment I am whatever I am and it's simple.

That night I go out with a Swedish guy, a German girl, and a couple of Aussies from the hostel. We find a local bar and buy round after round of shots, finding silly reasons to toast one another. This is the most normal thing I've done on this trip, and a part of me thinks, see? I'm still capable of drinking, talking, laughing; I'm still capable of being human. The other part of me—the part that detaches and watches and analyzes each moment—thinks, who do I think I'm fooling, as though the laughter, the *saluds*, the

drunken flush spreading across my cheeks is a ridiculous and transparent ruse, as though I've shown up
to a kegger dressed for a masquerade ball.

As the night progresses, we get drunker and the bar
gets busier. Unable to hear across the table, we break
into pairs for further conversation. I talk to the Swede,
Johann, who I met at the hostel the night before.
Johann is Swedish through and through—big and
bearded, inquisitive but mild, tri-lingual, and perhaps
a bit more outgoing than most Swedes, who tend to
take a while to warm up to people they don't know.
We talk about his dissertation on Scandinavian fairy
tales and I tell him that I used to write. At one point
he asks me, "So, what's your story? Why are you here?"

I think about giving him a canned response—oh,
just on summer vacation, or I've always wanted to
see the country. "My ancestors are Swedish," I say.
And I could stop right there, but I don't. "My dad
and I were supposed to take this trip together," I say.
"But he died." And I tell Johann about the ashes.

Johann lets this sink in and says, "That is not what
I was expecting you to say." For a minute he says
nothing. Then he nods as though we've concluded
our business and swivels his barstool toward Anna,
the German girl sitting on his left, and begins talking
with her. I turn to the right, to John the Aussie who

gracefully and immediately envelops me into the conversation he's having with the other Aussie. They're both drunk and boisterous, so all I have to do is laugh and nod as I think about how the information about my dad, how that information about myself, is a hot coal no one wants to touch, how those who get near it try to pass it off before it starts to burn. Johann doesn't want that information and I don't blame him. He lobbed it back to me as though to say, this is not what I asked for. Sitting there in the bar I decide that I must retain possession of that information and all its implications. After all, it belongs to me.

Malmö, Sweden

It's raining when I take the bus from Uppsala to Gothenburg, and still raining when I go from Gothenburg to Malmö. After I hang my sodden things in the hostel, I wander aimlessly along the canals and watch the rain puncture their surface. I walk through a carnival in the Moorish part of town. The carnival is closed and rain collects in the bucket seats of the Ferris wheel and the spinning tea cups. The rides and booths are splashed with psychedelic pink and purple swirls, grinning clowns, kaleido-scopes, posters for upcoming concerts. The empty carnival makes me want to weep. I imagine the lines and the sounds and the smells of a sunny day, yet at this moment, it seems entirely plausible that there will never be another sunny day, that these gears and motors will never again turn, that children will never race to climb aboard and strap themselves in. I walk through the carnival, circling each ride until I find myself standing in front of the merry-go-round. I picture my dad there, his hand on the small of my back as I cling to the long candy cane pole.

And there's this: I'm wandering around an abandoned carnival in the rain because a part of me believes that he's out here somewhere. Maybe not here, exactly—maybe he's under a waterfall in Croatia or in a market in Istanbul or floating down a fjord—but if I keep looking, on a day not so different from today, I'll find him.

Copenhagen, Denmark

The Danes, known as the happiest people in the world, lack the austerity of the Swedes. Many of them dress like they're in the Sex Pistols; even old men wear skinny black jeans and wallet chains. People sit in the main square with huge cans of beer and 20-inch hot dogs, and they ride bikes everywhere. There's an amusement park in the center of the city so that wherever you go, you can see the lights and the roller coasters threading the corkscrews and hear sounds of laughter.

There's a part of Copenhagen called Christiania, which spans four or five city blocks and calls itself a "free state" and retains sovereignty from the local, city, and national political structure. Its entrance is marked by phantasmagoric murals on the sides of buildings—fairies and daemons and other bug-eyed, marvelous creatures. Photographs are forbidden. There are some bars and restaurants, as well as a local industry—custom bike making. There are high wheelers, tandem and family bikes, bikes with motor-cycle sidecars, bikes with baby carriages attached to the front. It's legal to buy hash in Christiania, though its sale is much less public than it once was and operations are fairly hush hush. In the center of Christiania is a pavilion with dozens of picnic tables where people sit, talk, smoke, and play games that they borrow from one of the bars that form a loose circle around the edges.

I buy a beer and sit at an empty picnic table. Within minutes, an Italian guy with wonderfully idiosyncratic English sits down, opens a backgammon board, and asks me to play. My mom and I used to play backgammon in the evenings when I was little, but I haven't played in years. The game removes the pressure of conversation—we chat idly as we study the board. He asks where I'm from and I tell him Michigan, to which he responds, "Detroit?" I tell him Kalamazoo and he loves the word and repeats it over and over. Then, because he's wearing a baseball cap, I tell him I went to high school with Derek Jeter and he flips. He calls some friends, and within 15 minutes we've been joined by three other Italian guys and two Aussies.

Later that evening, after the Italians and Aussies leave, two women ask if they can sit with me. They are Sudanese; one is 19 and the other is 21. They speak four languages and in perfect English tell me the story of how their dad escaped Sudan to study in Egypt and then brought them and their mother to Kuwait and then to Denmark when the Gulf War started. These girls have a lot of questions about the U.S. They ask why kids are so angry that they go around shooting people at school. They ask about gun laws, socioeconomic divides, health care, vacation time. Rather than being anti-American, they seem honestly befuddled at our politics. We talk for hours and share food. When we leave, I realize that I haven't thought about my dad in at least an hour. I had an organic and rewarding experience without having to think or be or feel anything in particular, which proves that somewhere, underneath the confusion and the grief, I am intact and engaged and maybe even interesting and likable, still part of the world.

Bergen, Norway

Part of me wants to stay in Copenhagen forever, making daily pilgrimages to Christiania for board games and intoxicants and company that draws out the best of myself. If this were my life, I think, I'd be happy. Except I know that's not true. Christiania and Copenhagen make me happy because they're a sanctuary and a reprieve—they aren't meant to be the sites of my daily life. Still, leaving Copenhagen hurts. It's like leaving a new lover or friend behind, only I think the friend I'm leaving behind is me. As I travel to Bergen, reality descends again: my dad is dead, his ashes are in my bag, and I'm alone and still broken.

I ride the funicular to the mountaintop for a view of the whole city, the marketplace, the main square, the fountain. I feel like an alien descended from space watching people scurry about, trading reindeer pelts for baleen, sausage for fresh salmon, wool for knives. I've already forgotten how to interact with the people who live and breathe and walk next to me. I don't know how to negotiate the best price for mittens or pick the finest Norwegian cheese; I don't know how to throw Kroner in the fountain and make a wish without being overtaken by bitterness. Perhaps I was hasty in believing I was part of the human race.

Bergen is packed with families. Parents maneuver their children, each holding a hand, sometimes swinging the kids between them. My parents never spent much on cars or televisions or other goods—they pooled it all for trips. If they hadn't, I might not be here now. Watching the families reminds me of the vacations we used to take—camping in Northern Michigan, to the U.S. coasts, Canada, Hawaii, London. My mom, dad, brother and I always went on these trips, and my dad's parents usually joined us. Half of our vacation six-some is dead now. What kind of world allows that to happen? I think about having kids, and how they'll never get to go fishing with their grandpa; how my dad, who so loved to travel, will never be part of our vacation crew. They will never hold his hand and walk down the street.

I ride back down the funicular to the park in the city center, which has a small lake with a fountain whose shooting water catches sunlight and breaks it into colors that leap and fall. I sit on a bench near the water and toss potato chips to the geese. People walk dogs and amble arm in arm down the paths as though today is an ordinary day.

A father and daughter walk a spotted dog. They let it off the leash and split up, each hiding behind a tree. The dog barks and circles the park, ears perked like radio towers. The dog finds the girl and they run together, looking for the father. From behind an oak he tightropes shade and sun. He casts a long shadow. I can see him from here.

The girl playing hide and seek with her dad is the most beautiful thing I've ever seen. It hurts like a cut on a joint I can't avoid using, breaking open whenever I bend it. At the same time, dissolving into tears on this park bench is also a huge relief, like finally throwing up after struggling for hours to keep down something that hasn't agreed with you.

A woman stops and asks me something in Norwegian. She looks concerned. I nod and say, "I'm okay." She pauses, unconvinced. I give her a thumbs up sign and a weak smile. She shrugs and keeps going.

A couple months ago my therapist asked me when, where, and how I cried. After the requisite jokes ("I cry through my elbows—do you think there's something wrong with me?") I told her that I'd find a good time when I didn't have to be anywhere or do anything and then I'd make myself cry by playing the slideshow from Dad's memorial or listening to Sufjan Stevens or watching *E.T.* or some other sappy thing.

"So," she said, "you wait until it's convenient, set up a conducive and controlled environment behind closed doors, and then allow yourself to cry?"

It didn't sound quite so healthy when she put it that way. All the catharsis I allowed myself was premeditated and contained. I was so focused on being functional and strong that sometimes I worried that the grief would sneak up and overtake me, like a tidal wave. But here, away from my family, away from my life, I can acknowledge that I'm not okay. And, if I'm so inclined, I can freak out and get ugly. It's safer here than it ever was in my therapist's room or even in the privacy of my own apartment. For some reason, realizing that I can freak out makes me feel better.

Oslo, Norway

I ride a public bus on a rainy morning, watching Norwegians get on and shake off, stow their umbrellas neatly, smooth their fair hair. They're almost all dressed for work, sharp despite the rain, smart and confident in their arrangements. They like to read on the bus—the newspaper, books, briefs. All of them seem so secure in their movements, in their bodies, in their lives. I too drop my nose into a book, as much out of wanting to belong as out of actual inclination to read. As I tend to do during short spans of reading time, I read Whitman. This morning, he describes me:

> *Another self, a duplicate of every one,*
> *skulking and hiding as it goes,*
> *Formless and wordless...*
> *Keeping fair with the customs,*
> *speaking not a syllable of itself,*
> *Speaking of anything else, but never itself.*

I wander around Oslo's Vigeland sculpture garden in the rain, following the curves of palms and crooks of elbows that flow from one statue to another, figures embracing, creating shapes together, extending their limbs to children holding hands with other children. I see myself reflected in a statue of a woman contained entirely within a granite circle, wild-haired and caged and ready to break. From on top of statued stairs I look down to the bridge and see a mass of umbrellas bobbing against the grey in a chaos of color. There are people beneath those umbrellas, holding them up.

One of those people, an older woman, falls as she walks up a ramp. Her husband helps gather her up and she seems shaky but otherwise okay. My chest shrinks, cringes inward with recognition. My whole body remembers Dad falling. The Titanic of men, someone you'd think could never topple. How he fell like a child who simply couldn't understand how to avoid it, at odds with his own body. And though he was losing weight rapidly, shedding himself, when he fell it sounded like a redwood crashing.

I walk through the rain, crying. The fear that Dad's death might drown me has calmed; without a dam, there can be no rush of water. I've achieved some degree of emotional regularity. Everything is moving—the earth under my feet, my feet upon the earth, my thoughts, the grief inside of me. For the first time, I consider that it might be okay if hurt inhabits moments of joy and beauty, that they don't have to be at odds. All of it is going somewhere, moving, maybe even forward.

Riga, Latvia

It's my last night in Riga and I should go out and experience the nightlife, but I'm not in the mood to try and round up people at the hostel, nor am I in the mood to go somewhere alone, buy myself a drink, and watch people and write in my journal. As I'm debating what to do, the door opens and in walks an Indian guy who introduces himself with an adorable British accent as Avi. We get to talking and he invites me to go bar hopping with some other travelers.

Our group starts small—Avi and me and a couple of others, and by the third beer has grown to about a dozen. We're all reveling in the glories of travel and cheap beer and instant connections with strangers. As the night wears on, Avi asks me enough questions that it becomes cumbersome to avoid telling him the truth about this trip. Encouraged by a couple shots of Black Balsam liqueur, I tell him that my favorite person in the world is dead, that I've got his ashes in my bag, that this trip is a pilgrimage. Unlike Johann, Avi is intrigued by this bit of information; travelers who have done their own walkabouts often recognize the lonesome but dogged pursuit of self-knowledge and resurrection. Every now and then, travelers participate in some small way in the quest of others, even if it's just passing an evening exchanging stories.

I don't know if it's me, my story, or the booze that causes Avi to narrow his focus on me. The part of me that observes from a small distance what my physical body does knows exactly what's happening, knows what will happen. The part of me in the moment wants to get drunk and flirt and feel normal.

While I enjoy Avi and find him smart and funny, I don't have any feelings about him either way—I don't particularly want to kiss him, nor do I not want to kiss him. Motivated by alcohol and the overwhelming desire for normalcy, I decide to act the part anyway. We push our chairs into a darkened corner of the bar and make out. I keep feeling like everyone's watching us, but every time I look up, everyone is consumed by dancing, talking, flirting. Kissing Avi is okay; I don't love it, but I don't dislike it. I keep kissing him, partly to avoid talking, but mostly to avoid thinking. When his hands start moving across my body, the part of me outside myself is the first to notice. The me in the moment doesn't feel his palm crest the ridge of my knee; the outside me watches his fingers slide to my inner thigh.

We leave in a rush of paying and gathering and kissing and groping. The me on the outside is impressed—if I didn't know better, I'd think that the me tangled in the arms of this man was utterly consumed. The me in those arms is simply there, spending moments like loose change. We duck into an alleyway and tuck ourselves into a shadow.

He's murmuring in my ear; I'm more conscious of his accent than I am of his fingers under my shirt, climbing my ribs, lifting my tanktop with the back of his hands. My eyes trace the curving lines of a balcony that perfectly exemplifies Riga's famous art nouveau architecture. The outside me sees my fingers edge around Avi's back, crawling the length of his spine, playing it like a piano. The outside me can't see his fingers between the press of our bodies, so it takes a while for me to realize that he's freed buttons and parted zippers, to hear the soft plastic sound of a condom wrapper. When I do notice, I have no reaction. There's nothing to see here. My body keeps moving, hips tilted, legs wrapping around the back of his thighs. I watch from a distance, head slightly tilted, curious and surprised but somehow not that surprised, and I think well, this makes as much sense as anything, I suppose.

And then the me in the moment has the clearest thought I've had all night: Dad knows that I'm having sex with a stranger in an alley in Latvia.

Once it pops into my mind, the thought latches onto me like a trap I can't shake loose. I've felt Dad's presence on this trip and in many other moments, mostly when I want him to see and know what's happening. If he's somehow aware of those moments, how can he not be conscious of everything else? I don't get to pick and choose—if he's here at all, in any form, he can see everything. Shame burns through the drunkenness, through the movements of our loose joints. I open my eyes to see if Avi notices, but his cheek is pressed against mine, he's still speaking softly into my ear, another language now. Burying my face into his neck, I hide from the people stumbling home, from my dad, from the outside me. The me in this moment wants now to disappear inside of it. I breathe in the humid air escaping the crush of our bodies, looking for flecks of light between our skin, passages, the way back.

I can't sleep, aware of Avi in a bunk across the room, aware of the jar in my pack as though it houses something living, something that needs to breathe, aware that Dad is close. I get up and pack my things slowly and silently in the dark. I head to the bus station and buy a new ticket for a seat on the first bus of the day. I wait in the station. The fluorescent overhead lights of the bus station flicker, soundtracked by the punctuated brush of pushbrooms across the gritty floor. There are a few other people in the station. A couple is dead asleep, slumped together. The rest are zoned out, staring at walls, staring at nothing, perhaps drunk or high, perhaps trapped in the intricacies of their minds.

Something about a bus station in the early hours of the morning bares the truth. Everyone in the station, in sleep or intoxication or solipsism, submits to a visible vulnerability, hiding nothing under those quivering spotlights.

I sleep fitfully on the bus to Estonia, images flashing into my head that might be memories or dreams. Last night, even though it doesn't sit wonderfully with me by the light of day, is what it is, and for better or for worse, I'm pressing on. Still on walkabout, still trying to meet back up with myself again. In five hours, I'll be in another country, and who knows what I'll be.

Tallinn, Estonia

Tallinn makes me feel instantly better. It's quainter than Riga, less flashy, fewer dark alleys. There's a medieval wall around the heart of the city and I follow it up a hill to a park, splashed in light, dappled by sun. I feel rejuvenated—the rapid transition from Riga to here, the aesthetic of this place, its loveliness. I walk around all day and much of the night, comfortable, and not wanting to stop, knowing that discomfort is out there and thinking that if I can keep moving it won't catch up to me. But it never closes in, and I want to pat Tallinn on the shoulder, thank it for making me feel close to okay, for having become something of a friend. Wordlessly and without being asked, a city can give me all I need in a moment or a day—it can look into my eyes and measure my footfalls and know why I've come. And I figure that in these places, I'm more likely than anywhere else to cross paths with myself.

Helsinki, Finland

Whitman says, "To look up or down no road but it stretches and waits for you—however long, but it stretches and waits for you."

I take the ferry from Tallinn to Helsinki and I know within five minutes that Helsinki speaks to me. As I walk to the hostel, I feel loose, unleashed upon the world, full of equal parts potential and kinetic energy. The weather here is nicer by far than anywhere else on this trip, which in conjunction with the crackling energy of this city underscores my feeling that there is joy to experience here.

I rent a bike and ride around for a day, visiting sites

in the city center like the marketplace where I try fried silver fish and fresh lingonberries and watch the fisherman haul in their catches. A Finnish man with a face weathered like the deck of an old boat carves bears out of balsam. I ride to the beach, to the Olympic Stadium, to the Sibelius monument, which looks like the guts of a pipe organ suspended in the air. At first I bike with my map folded strategically in the basket so I can see where I'm going. Before long, I'm off the map and I get tired of stopping to check my position. I put the map away and ride, figuring that if I get lost I can ask for directions or keep riding until I find myself again. The freedom from an agenda and a destination turns the pedals along with my feet, turns my face toward the fresh salt breeze, giving me a feeling of being not on wheels but on air, winged and triumphant over gravity.

The water helps me navigate—I curve with it, hugging the shore. Near a peninsula that looks to be a series of loading docks, I happen to glance up at a street sign that reads: Ehrenströmintie. Renstrom means "from the water," so it's not terribly surprising that a street name would incorporate our name, but the significance of me happening upon this street feels immeasurable. Here is my name, his name, alive half a world away, a road traversed by locals and by travelers, a route to the sea.

The hostel in Helsinki is one of the best. Among other things, they have a library where travelers can swap books, as well as huge overstuffed reading chairs positioned by the windows. Each evening I go back to the hostel and read, sometimes also cooking dinner in the cozy kitchen next to the reading room. Perhaps it's Helsinki, perhaps it's this hostel, and just maybe it's got something to do with me, but it's easy to strike up conversations with other travelers here, to recommend books, swap stories, fall into chopping vegetables and putting gigantic pots of water to boil on the stove for ubiquitous travelers' pasta.

I talk with Simon, who's from Switzerland and has perfect, lilting English. I noticed him on my first night here when I saw the way he handled the book he was reading, how he turned the pages slowly and gently, as though time for him had stopped. He studies pages the way a boy studies the shining back of a beetle, as though the words in his hands are precious and alive. Tonight I bring out the beat up copy of Whitman so I can watch the way he cradles its spine and runs his fingers over the print. As I chop cucumbers for salad, I hear him reading softly, the gentle slopes of his accent pushing murmurs of words above the steam:

I will scatter myself among men and women as I go;

I will toss the new gladness and roughness among them;

I slow the knife on the tomatoes, pause so I can listen.

…Here the profound lesson of reception, neither preference or denial;

They pass—I also pass—anything passes—none but are accepted…

He glances up, sees me listening.

I think whatever I shall meet on the road I shall like,

and whoever beholds me shall like me.

"I like this Walt Whitman," he says, his W's sounding like soft V's.

Later that night I go out with Simon and a few other people from the hostel to a local vodka bar. The easy energy of the city transforms at night into good-natured rowdiness, rounds of shots for others, dancing to bad Finnish pop. They ask me the same questions as everyone else I've met; I tell them that I'm from Michigan, that I'm 29, that I own a cat, that I'm a teacher, that I was in NYC on September 11, that I've been traveling in Scandinavia for a few weeks.

The words and stories about myself sound and feel different—they do not fall broken from my lips, and when I'm finished talking, there sits before me an empty glass, rather than an empty seat. When we break off into smaller conversations, I tell Simon that I write. He tells me that making books smells like hot tea.

As we walk back to the hostel after the bars close, Simon reaches for my hand. I concentrate on the slight swing of his arm, on his warm palm, the way he holds my hand as though I'm a normal person. I feel a glowing ache spread through me; this is the first time I've actually wanted to touch someone since Dad died.

We sit out on the balcony of the hostel, looking at the stars and talking. I feel as though I've aged a decade since someone put his arms around me like this. The solid warmth of him makes me want to sob. When we kiss, it's with none of the urgent fumblings of the encounter with Avi in the dark alleyway—it's gentle yet assured, unhurried, somehow expansive. At one point I find myself thinking about Dad watching and decide that even if he is, he could have no complaints about this timeless kiss and its countless gestures of deliverance. Simon's hands tangle in my hair and caress my scalp, as though massaging the memories there. I keep my eyes closed, my mind dotted with stars, and feel the calluses of the press on his fingertips, the quiet, complicated prints.

Hedemora, Sweden

Today's the day I've been awaiting and dreading, the culmination and the end, my goodbye. I can't believe this trip is nearing completion, that he's still gone. Part of me was really expecting to find him, or at least some sign. Hedemora's the last opportunity to find him, or whatever it is I'm looking for.

The town is quite small, and after I check into the only hostel I head straight to the library to find some information about where Dad's ancestors lived, or some other place or detail they incorporated into their lives. After searching online and in countless town registries and censuses with the help of a few kind librarians, I'm confronted with the possibility that I won't be able to find any part of him or his ancestry, that I won't know where to put his ashes.

I leave the library and walk to the cemetery, which is impeccably manicured yet sprawling. There's a small church on the grounds; I walk in and light a candle for Dad, tears swimming in front of the flame. Then I stroll each and every path on the grounds, scanning the names on the headstones for anything that looks vaguely familiar. So many beloved in the ground, so many families split by death then reunited in burial, so many flowers and inscriptions and prayers. None of them ours.

When it gets dark I hole up in a pub—I don't know what else to do. I'm nearly paralyzed by the profundity of this last symbolic act; I don't know how, when or where to finish but I have to figure it out soon. I'm due to leave Hedemora tomorrow evening. I stare into my beer, watching the particles settle and bubble, thinking and not thinking, trying to pry the weight off.

By the next morning I've given up on the idea of one perfect place; no single place could contain him. I spread his ashes in a few places—first, Lake Hönsan, a small lake lined by reeds and spotted with lillypads, whose flowers burst like small suns from the clear blue water, soundtracked by the lazy squabbling of ducks and the contented echo of belching frogs. I kneel down by the water and take the jar out of my bag. I unwrap it as if I'm unwrapping a new piece of glassware. Without pausing or hurrying, I open the jar and hold it above the water. I watch my hand tip it sideways, slowly, until the ashes slide to the lip of the jar and then instantly scatter when they drop into the air, taken away, absorbed into the ether.

I spread about 20 percent of his ashes, then close the jar and stow it away. I take a couple of pictures and write down in my journal something I love about Dad, something he loved about me, and some kind of goal or promise for the future. I connect myself to the future and to him via some trait of mine and resolve to cultivate the qualities that he loved about me, which almost invariably are the things that I appreciate about myself. After I finish, the ducks are still bobbing for greens and the dragonflies continue chasing one another, the filaments of their wings turned to metallic rainbows in the sun.

I go to a nature preserve with towering evergreens. I make a tall pile of flat, rust-colored rocks and spread more ashes there. Again, I take a picture and write in my journal. I do the same thing at Lake Brunnsjön, which curves around Hedemora like a kidney bean and is flanked by sloping hills, which are buffeted by clouds that burst forward like locomotive steam. I walk out to the marshy parts where leggy birds stand and old rowboats float among the cattails. The burn of anger dampens and the angst and anxiety break like a fever. I no longer feel as though I've swallowed a firecracker.

The last place is the cemetery. As I continue naming

the important pieces of myself and setting goals for the future, it becomes abundantly clear that Dad will not be in it. But I do it anyway, because what is there to do but move ahead into that future? I don't empty the jar—I keep a little bit for Stockholm, a city to which I feel more connected and think he would have, too.

Stockholm , Sweden

A few hours before my flight back to the States I walk back to Södermalm, to the cliff that overlooks the city. It's windy, a crabby wind that gusts then quiets then kicks back up. Dark clouds gather and part in the sky over the spire of the Stockholm cathedral's tower. It's strange to think that I stood in this very spot five weeks ago. How long ago that seems, how it feels like I've aged 10 years since then, like I've finished a dozen marathons on end.

I climb over the railing and kneel on a small outcropping of land. I'm sobbing before I get the jar out of my bag. My mind is empty of thoughts, yet full of fuzzy noise. I open the jar and turn it upside down. The wind spirits the ashes away before I have a chance to register it. I sit there dumbly, crying into the wind, thinking and feeling a million things but also not thinking or feeling any of them. I leave the jar, open, on a flat slab of rock.

Then, in the kind of moment that only happens in the movies, the clouds above the cathedral part and reveal a silhouette of sun and a rainbow arching over the city. I take pictures, hardly believing what I'm seeing, wanting evidence. In my head, I talk to my dad. I do not ask if he's there or if he can hear me. I tell him that Barack Obama is going to win the primary, that I love Scandinavia and the fact that we're from here, that it all makes sense. I tell him that I'm teaching and taking care of his things at the office and at home. I tell him that I miss him, that I love him, and that I'll be okay.

Scandinavian Air flight 614

I read "Song of an Open Road" again on the plane. This time, a new line leaps out at me that I want to cup in my palms and never let go: "I am larger, better than I thought; I did not know I held so much goodness." I think about what goodness is, what it means. I decide that this trip was good.

We soar over the edge of the world. Slices of cloud float in our wake, silent. I become aware of my reflection in the window and soon I can only see my face when I look out at the water. It doesn't seem to belong to me, this face in the mirror. There are two of me—the home me and the away me. The home me is the one that separates from my body and watches, the one that has to schedule a good cry, the one who feels as blandly empty as a sagging balloon. The home me spends hours online looking for places to visit, keeps track of air fares, repeatedly checks the status of frequent flyer miles; the home me devotes a great deal of time to getting away from home, to transitioning into the away me. I miss the away me when she's gone. I try to emulate her bravery but often find that I don't know how. The away me reminds the rest of me who I want to be, who I can be. I look for her a lot.

How many millions of events and moments had to occur to bring me here, suspended between home and away, before and after, between continents? I imagine the plane suddenly plummeting, the sensation of freefall. I want to like that feeling; I want to be good at it. I don't have control over the world or the whims of life, just as I don't have control over whether this plane stays in the air. Yet here I am, on this plane, in this world, riding along wherever it goes, still moving.

Fighting the Sunday Blues
with Albert Camus

"As if that blind rage had washed me clean,
rid me of hope; for the first time, in that night
alive with signs and stars, I opened myself to
the gentle indifference of the world."
Albert Camus, *The Stranger*

The Sunday blues are back, familiar and unwelcome like the symptoms of an old illness.

Sundays became my nemesis in high school, especially the nights, which I'd spend biting my nails and lying sleeplessly in bed, cataloging all that was wrong with my life. I asked myself more depressing questions about my future on Sunday nights than at any other time.

The current relapse of the Sunday blues is even worse. Now, instead of attending high school, I teach there. When Sunday night rolls around, I feel as though I'm being forced into the spotlight in front of a tough crowd, and there's nowhere to hide.

The toughest crowd is my senior World Literature

class—17 students, five of whom require special modifications and accommodations. The students' range of skills and interests runs the gamut, but most aren't big fans of reading and none of them likes to write. My most recent attack of the Sunday blues is exacerbated knowing that the next morning, I have to explain absurdism and introduce Camus' *The Stranger*.

"What do you mean, life has no meaning?" they ask. The emo kids smirk at each other—they've known this forever. I pose some classic existential questions: why are we here? What is our purpose in life? What are we meant to do? I tell them that Camus thinks there is no purpose or meaning for humans, that our efforts at finding meaning inevitably fail, and are thus absurd. They stare at me emptily.

"So basically, you go with the flow," I say.

In the following days, my students saunter into class after the bell, insisting that it's better than rushing, or that they were too busy going with the flow to finish chapter three. I interpret this as a good sign—it's better than silence, or that lobotomized stare.

As I reread *The Stranger*, the book feels like a personal message from Camus about the past couple years of my life—my struggle to come to terms with the death of my father, spinning in the hamster wheel trying to figure out why he died and what his death suggests about the way the universe works (or doesn't). What did it *mean* that I spent the two years after his death in my hometown of Kalamazoo, that I turned 30 in the same place I was born, that I had no idea what to do with my life.

In those two years back in Michigan, I found no answers to my questions. Largely because I believed my search for meaning wouldn't yield anything in Kalamazoo, I moved to Boston, which seemed to hold more promise, stones yet unturned. Initially, the novelty consumed me, but after a few weeks, the questions returned, along with the Sunday blues.

Camus would say that I didn't find the answers because the answers don't exist. He may be right.

In *The Stranger*, Meursault responds very differently to his mother's death than I did to my father's: "Maman died today. Or yesterday maybe, I don't know." He simply doesn't react, and is more concerned about coffee and the brightness of the sun. My suffering over the unfairness of my dad's death would have struck Camus as pointless. I couldn't have responded like Meursault, but I recognize the wisdom in his response. The human condition is one of mortality, so death isn't sad or unfair or surprising—

it just *is*. Death is inevitable, but sadness is not.

My students, though, go to great lengths to explain Meursault's response to his mother's death, and his general lack of affect. "He's in shock," they say. "He's numb." They don't care if the text doesn't support these theories; they can't accept the idea that Meursault's mother's death doesn't mean anything to him. They persist in assigning humanity to Meursault because he makes them uncomfortable. What kind of person is he, they ask—which raises the question: is Meursault human? Suddenly, we find ourselves in the midst of a real conversation. The glazed looks are gone and hands wave in the air.

The book gives the students new ideas to consider and to rail against; they want to prove Camus wrong. They search for meaning in a book that celebrates life's meaninglessness. "You're making us read this book, so it must mean something," someone half-jokes. "And you tell us that this class has meaning, so that'd better be true, too."

Unlike my students, I find myself attracted to absurdism, at least intellectually, largely because it asserts the pointlessness of angst and dread. I'm attracted to the simplicity—the idea that what happens happens, and has no larger meaning. There's no reason to get caught up in anything because it isn't important; we aren't important. But I can't tell these teenagers, whom I'm supposed to encourage to dream big, that we—that they—aren't important.

My students desperately want Meursault to snap out of it. Even after he shoots the Arab for no reason at all, or, as he says in court, "because of the sun," they're heartened when he experiences discomfort at being labeled a criminal—he recognizes, even if only temporarily, the meaning that label carries. There's even a moment when Meursault has "the stupid urge to cry, because [he] could feel how much all these people hated [him]." For a beat, Meursault is recognizably human. But it doesn't last. When the chaplain visits him in prison, Meursault not only rejects God, but insists on life's meaninglessness. Ultimately, Meursault can't escape the consequences assigned to the meaning society has given life, because those consequences include his death. However, he does succeed in asserting his absurdist world view until his execution.

Despite their feelings of discomfort regarding Meursault I suggest to my students that because Meursault remains true to himself and to his beliefs, and because he thwarts society's attempt to impose its values onto him, he's a hero—at least, in Camus' eyes. This makes the class squirm. They ask how a murderer can be a hero. It's a question so reasonable that it seems almost rhetorical. But more importantly, it's an opening; the best teaching moments come from flipping the obvious, subverting the expected.

My students understand that we're going someplace heady and strange and possibly uncomfortable. Some of them actually rub their temples. But most of them are game to see where this leads. Curiosity indicates receptivity; a few have said that this is the most bizarre book they've ever read, that they'll keep reading if only to see how much stranger it gets.

Camus, I tell them, claims we have three choices once we realize that the search for meaning is absurd: we can commit suicide, take a leap of faith or accept life's meaninglessness. Upon realizing life's meaninglessness, most people either kill themselves or invest in God. Camus rejects suicide because it's a concession that life isn't worth living, and he considers putting all of one's eggs in the God basket an irrational and desperate attempt to find meaning. Camus suggests instead that we should accept life's absurdity and enjoy the freedom and peace to be found in the absence of meaning. It doesn't matter if Meursault moves to Paris or stays in Algiers, if he marries Marie, or if Raymond beats his girlfriend. It doesn't matter if Meursault kills a man, or if he's put to death. Meursault emerges as a true nonconformist because he doesn't just revel in absurdity—he actually creates personal meaning by embracing it.

"Sometimes, our conversations go like this," one of the students says, tracing an infinity sign in the air. They still like the idea of going with the flow, and a couple of them consider Meursault a badass. They follow Camus' logic to a point—they too reject suicide, and, interestingly, most of them reject the leap of faith, which leaves only door number three.

"But it's not like you have to go kill a guy because the sun's in your eyes," they say. "So you accept life's absurdity. What does that *mean?*"

"Well, nothing," I say, "which is kind of the point." But no one can deny that Camus' philosophy has big implications. What resonates with me is Camus' argument that accepting life's lack of meaning grants total freedom—freedom from destiny, from society, from personal fears and desires. This freedom allows us to define ourselves, and to give life the meaning it doesn't inherently have.

Maybe because they're minors who have to go to school, they can't really grasp the concept of total freedom. Maybe I can't really grasp it either: it's precisely this freedom that scares me about having moved to Boston. Before, the limitations of

Kalamazoo held me back, or that's what I told myself. Now, nothing holds me back from the answers I've been looking for. So where does this leave me, other than sleepless on a Sunday night, again?

Sartre defines dread as the fear of nothing. The classic example is the man who is afraid of falling off a cliff, but is also afraid he might throw himself off because nothing is holding him back. Boston is my proverbial cliff: now that nothing's holding me back, I can do anything. I can also do nothing, and this time I can't blame it on geography. I wonder whether the Sunday blues reflect the challenges of the classroom or my fear of the freedom gained by my move. Regardless of the answer, staring over the edge of the cliff doesn't change anything, except perhaps to make me unhappy.

I ask the students whether Meursault is happy. Most of them start off saying no. How could he be? He doesn't love anyone, he doesn't care if he or anyone else lives or dies. But, they clarify, Meursault does seem content when he eats a nice cut of sausage or takes a nap in the sun or has sex with Marie. I ask them to articulate the difference between being content in the moment and being happy. What does it mean to be happy? One student points out that being happy doesn't *mean* anything—happy just is, and you either feel it or you don't, which is why Meursault pursues physical pleasure. Pleasure is a natural bodily response—there's no thinking or meaning involved. So perhaps Meursault is happy after all.

The students sit with that, foreheads wrinkled, noses scrunched as if there's a bad smell in the room.

Maybe we should ask ourselves why we're uncomfortable with the idea that he's happy, I suggest. Some of the students, mostly guys, lower their eyes. Others, mostly girls, raise their hands. "We don't want him to be happy," one says. "He doesn't deserve it," someone else says. "We don't really like him," another admits. I'm impressed at their insight and candor despite the fact that they're proving Camus' point by imposing their own values onto Meursault. Even though Meursault is morally questionable, if not arguably reprehensible, I still want them to be able to understand his point of view. I want them to make judgments based on knowledge, but more than anything, I want them to be capable of compassion, even toward the strange or the unsavory.

"Get this," I say: "Camus claims that happiness is the brother of absurdism." Pause. "You know how I say that you can make the craziest argument in the world, as long as you back it up?" Another pause.

"Don't you want to know how Camus backs it up?" The question is rhetorical—I'm already pulling a stack of handouts from a folder.

I pass out an excerpt from Camus' "The Myth of Sisyphus," the essay in which he first defined absurdism. "Happiness and the absurd are two sons of the same earth. They are inseparable. It would be a mistake to say that happiness necessarily springs from the absurd discovery. It happens as well that the feeling of the absurd springs from happiness."

"Can you see how acceptance of absurdism—the relief of not having to make sense of anything—might be joy?" I ask. Their faces go blank. "Stay with me," I say. "Let's talk about Sisyphus."

"This poor dude has to push a boulder up a mountain forever?" someone asks. I nod. They spend a few minutes trying to find a loophole. Perhaps Sisyphus can make it to the top when the gods aren't looking. I tell them that the punishment is a curse, that the boulder always rolls back down, that Sisyphus's task is eternal.

"Harsh," they say.

Despite Sisyphus' endless punishment, Camus argues that "the struggle itself toward the heights is enough to fill a man's heart. One must imagine

Sisyphus happy." How can Sisyphus possibly be happy? they ask. They insist that he's way worse off than Meursault. I explain that Sisyphus is happy because he has embraced his circumstance—he doesn't wish to do or be anything else. Because he has an eternal task, he's free from asking himself what's next, or what his purpose in life is. He has a purpose, and he creates his own meaning simply by pushing the boulder. The journey is the destination. "Sisyphus goes with the flow," one says. "He actually likes it," someone else marvels.

Camus' argument is sound, beautifully written, and compelling. But looking at the graphic of Sisyphus and his boulder on the handout makes me sad on a gut level, and no matter what Camus says, that does mean something. I realize I've drawn a line—I can only go with the flow so far. There's something to be said for changing course, for turning upstream.

Instead of writing essays on *The Stranger*, the students stage Meursault's retrial. Meursault can't deny that he shot the Arab, so the trial focuses on whether the shooting was premeditated and what the appropriate sentence should be. There are three lawyers on each side, four witnesses, a jury, and I'm the judge.

When the lawyers badger the kid playing Meursault,

he's all shrugs. The mild tone in which he describes shooting the Arab because the sun was in his eyes suggests rationality and lack of remorse. Marie fakes tears on the stand, admitting that Meursault doesn't really love her. The kid playing Raymond looks appropriately sketchy. Then, from out of nowhere, the defense argues that Meursault is crazy—that either he's not grieving because he's insane, or that grief has driven him mad. He needs help, they say.

I'm frustrated that they still don't understand that Meursault acts of his own volition. I exercise judicial prerogative and ask Meursault if he thinks there's anything wrong with him. He says no. "Do you want to change?" I ask. He shrugs and says, "No, why would I?" The jurors exchange glances and the defense glares at me. But in the end, even though it wasn't presented as an option, the jury finds Meursault insane and elects to send him to a facility for treatment.

When the jurors explain their decision, I realize that it's not because they don't understand Camus; rather, they reject absurdism. And so do I.

Although our rational minds may protest, we find Meursault's pursuit of sensual pleasure lacking—sleeping, swimming, sex, smoking, eating, drinking—it's all momentary and physical, and allows for no intimacy or real connection with others. He doesn't strive for anything more, and although he's okay with that, we're not.

More than that, absurdism is a rejection of hope. This is why the crucial moment for Sisyphus comes as he walks down the mountain, before his next ascent. He doesn't wish that the next ascent will be the last; he doesn't pray that the boulder will stay at the top the next time. Sisyphus is free of hope. Because Sisyphus cannot refuse his eternal task, any hope of it ending or changing is pointless, and will only bring misery. This rejection of hope allows Sisyphus—and Meursault, as he awaits his death in jail—to accept his situation, and that acceptance is what generates his ability to live, to keep pushing, and to be happy.

The jury sends Meursault to an institution because they still have hope for him, even if he has none for himself. As inhuman as Meursault seems, they find compassion for him, and in so doing, create meaning that not only surprises me, but actually applies to my life outside of the classroom. I feel a twinge of sadness as I collect their copies of *The Stranger*, but it's quickly replaced by anticipation when I pull the next book on the syllabus, *The Metamorphosis*, from the shelf.

How I Spent My Free Will

> "'None of you will go to America, none of
> you will be film stars. And none of you will be
> working in supermarkets…You were brought
> into this world for a purpose, and your futures,
> all of them, have been decided.'"
> Kazuo Ishiguro, *Never Let Me Go*

Marcus Price raises his hand for the first time in five months when I ask what happened in the chapter they were supposed to read last night for homework. It's a ghost, this arm floating up into the air, pale and limp from lack of use. I almost miss it, almost mistake it for a stray hair across my line of sight.

"Ruth died!" Marcus says.

A smattering of applause across the class.

In my head, the echo: "or was it yesterday…."

I didn't plan Kazuo Ishiguro's *Never Let Me Go* as a contrapuntal follow-up to *The Stranger*, but here it is. After the class's surprising engagement with Camus's philosophical stance, largely because it makes so much sense, we're reading a book that has an entirely different take on the way we grapple with life like unholy wrestlers, trying to force it into something with recognizable meaning.

Ishiguro deftly builds and then reveals the central mystery of *Never Let Me Go*; something is off at Hailsham, the boarding school that serves as the novel's setting and, like the students, the reader knows that the students aren't being told everything. About a third of the way through the book we learn that the students are clones and that after graduation they will begin donating their organs to "normal" humans and will die before they're thirty. Ishiguro lays down at the feet of the characters and the reader one unsettling truth after another, turning quiet into disquiet and then into a suckerpunch that delivers an exquisite hurt.

Never Let Me Go trades blow for philosophical blow with *The Stranger*. I picture Camus sitting on my right shoulder. "We're all going to die some day," he says, breezy as autumn. "It doesn't matter if or how much we hurt."

Ishiguro sits on my left shoulder. "Yes, we're all going to die someday," he says mildly. "Thus, how we hurt is the only thing that matters."

Camus left Algeria to hang out with the counter-cultural artistic and philosophical revolutionaries and ex pats of mid-century Paris; I didn't expect him to look like James Dean. His hair's combed back with pomade and he's smoking with rugged and somehow entirely un-ironic panache. He's wearing a navy pea coat with a popped collar over a button-up shirt and tie. He's also wearing black skinny jeans, which I realize is a historical inaccuracy, but who am I to question?

Ishiguro has wire-rimmed glasses and looks like a grown-up, Asian Harry Potter. His hair, parted shaggily down the middle, spills into his eyes; he constantly brushes it back but it's just shy of hooking behind his ears. And even though he doesn't have one in the picture on the back of the book, the Ishiguro on my shoulder has a carefully groomed moustache that rides his lip close, as if it knows a secret.

"Hurting is pointless. It doesn't change anything," Camus says.

"Maybe it's not supposed to change anything," Ishiguro says. Even though I know he grew up in the UK, his British accent catches me off guard, and, I have to admit, suggests credibility.

Camus takes a haughty drag from his cigarette.

Ishiguro coughs into my ear. It tickles.

* * *

Back to Marcus. Back to Ruth dying. Back before that, actually, to Ruth's final gesture and last wish.

Before Ruth dies, she apologizes to Kathy and Tommy, the main characters who realize they love each other too late to do much good about it, for keeping them apart. She says it should've been those two together all along, that she knew it when she dated Tommy. After she apologizes, she gives them the address of the headmistress, Madame, so they can find her and ask for the lovers' deferral—a couple of years to be together before they "complete."

On a tiny scrap of paper, Ruth gives them hope.

We discuss whether Ruth's act is virtuous or cruel— she puts an improbable idea into Tommy and Kathy's heads and the reader cringes, knowing how this is going to turn out, but nonetheless hoping that these characters will somehow get what they want. Tommy and Kathy invest in the deferral—they prepare for the visit, gather evidence of their love, and rehearse arguments for why they deserve the brief reprieve. They hope so hard that they genuinely buy into the fantasy of their own dreams and futures. Then they learn that the deferral is only a persistent rumor and that it doesn't exist.

The question, then, is whether Kathy and Tommy would have been better off if they had never believed in the deferral, if they'd never experienced false hope. In promoting this hope, did Ruth give them a gift or did she dangle a carrot cruelly out of reach?

I write on the board:

> either you get what you hope for

or

> you don't

It occurs to me that I've never articulated hope quite this simply before, reduced to two possible outcomes.

"Everything's fifty-fifty. Either something will happen or it won't," Camus says, flipping a franc on his knee. "This is why hoping is at best a pointless waste of time and at worst a guarantee of unhappiness. Either way, it separates us from the moment."

Not in front of the kids, I think. Standing under fluorescent lights in front of 20 teenagers isn't the ideal setting for an imaginary conversation with two famous writers.

In my periphery, I catch sight of Sam Connell; the deep weariness in his eyes reminds me of a lost and hungry puppy. Week after week, he describes in his reader response journal a web of connections between the book and the darkness of his own life. I'm glad that he's connecting to the book, though I'm worried that its weight will tug him under, that he'll have trouble kicking to the surface with it. Sam watches me intently. I think he wants me to argue for hope; I think he wants to be convinced. And I want desperately to convince him.

The problem is, I'm thinking about my dad and what it was like to believe, for moments here and there, that he would make it, that everything would be okay. I'm thinking about what it was like to be wrong.

Camus pokes my earlobe with the filter of his cigarette. "Move on with the lesson! Talk about how sappy ol' Ishi here is or something. Wade about in your sentimental drivel on your own time."

"The death of a parent—a favorite subject of yours, no?" Ishiguro says.

"When treated with a...certain touch, perhaps."

"Teacher second, human being first," Ishiguro says, running his hand through the part in his hair.

"Were you always this touchy-feely?" Camus loosens his tie.

"*Mono no aware*," Ishiguro says. "Pathos. Empathy. It's what separates us from animals.

You should try it sometime."

I feel Camus shrug. "Whatever you say, monsieur." He leans back and props his feet on my collarbone.

* * *

There wasn't one specific moment when we lost hope in Dad's recovery, at least not that I can identify. The sense of urgency in his care evaporated, replaced by a somber but firm efficiency that, in retrospect, made it clear that the doctors lost hope before we did. The oncologist withdrew Dad from the clinical trial. The surgeon told us that even removal of the entire colon wouldn't work, that the cancer had spread too far. The internist reviewed the latest CAT scan and quietly canceled all subsequent ones. The hospitalist had a new vocabulary: pain management, hospice, palliative care. I don't remember which of these moments was the one. I do remember that, like a cooling ember met suddenly with fierce breath, our hope would for an instant be reignited by a new treatment option, a firm hand on the shoulder, a twinkle shooting like a star across Dad's eyes.

At some point we all knew there was no hope. He was going to die, and soon. There was nothing to be done. There was no tiny scrap of paper. And we had to live with that, breathe it, make room for it in all the conversations we had with one another, with the nurses, and with whatever gods we might have supplicated to in the moments when it made sense to try divinity one more time. All the food we choked down, all the times we brushed our teeth, all the funny movies we pretended to watch—all of it with a crushing absence of hope.

What's left if you renounce hope?

"Everything," says Camus.

"Nothing," says Ishiguro.

Absence of hope takes many shapes. It's not the quiet and muted scarcity of something wonderful and luxurious, like chocolates or soft sheets. The absence of hope is the absence of something utterly essential. The absence of hope crumples your chest like cellophane. How ugly the world becomes when the clouds hang hopeless, how suffocating and stagnant. Nothing will ever move or change again. The clouds sag lower and lower until they bind you up like a beetle in a spider's web, unable even to contemplate the possibility of escape. You walk through days as though you're in a CGI movie; some grey shadow has filled your soul, digitally grafted over your image so that you look and feel sooty, dirty, damaged.

"Could you be any more maudlin?" Camus asks. "With your storm clouds and your poor excised heart." He cracks his knuckles one by one, saving his thumbs for last. "Your dad died. I died. You'll die. Sooner, later, with or without all your angst. So much useless angst. What are the angsty kids called these days?"

"Emo," says Ishiguro from around the back of my head, his breath skeeting my neck.

"Ah, yes. Emo." Camus chuckles. "I like that. There's nothing wrong with wearing all black—I've been known to slink about at parties in a black cat suit—but the whole black soul thing? I suppose it's vaguely silly, but all that pointless wallowing makes me want to *degorge*." He sticks a finger into his mouth and gags.

"You're a real piece of work," Ishiguro says.

Camus smiles. "*D'accord*, Emo."

"I will say this, though—the way we die is as important as the way we live."

"And then some." Camus lights another cigarette. "Death is what defines us. It's the most genuine experience we have. Besides this, of course." He takes a long drag and exhales theatrically.

"So we almost agree on something," Ishiguro says, wiping his hand across his forehead. "Except I don't think we actually need to die in order to experience something real. Mortality provides a lifelong and life-shaping invitation to examination and contemplation. It's a state of being—not just an event."

Camus sighs. "I don't suppose you'd be interested in a game of chess, would you?"

* * *

The day after we read chapter seven, in which Miss Lucy, a guardian at Hailsham, stops the students from fantasizing about their futures by telling them in no uncertain terms that their "lives are set out for [them]" and that in a few years they will begin donating their organs to "normals," my students squirm in their seats and hands stick up in the air before everyone's arrived in the room. "You mean that they're all going to donate their organs?" someone asks.

"Wait a minute...." One student after another tries to clarify.

"Until they die?"

"How is that possible?"

"Can't the students refuse?"

"Why are the guardians allowing this?"

"Why are the doctors and hospitals allowing this?"

"Does the government know? How can they allow this?"

"Who needs all those organs, anyway? What's happened?"

Even though they've gotten answers to some of the book's central questions, my students realize there's more that they don't know and perhaps don't want to know. They're uncomfortable with the knowledge they've just received; they want to give it back. They don't want to know that these kids were created with a specific fate and purpose—death. But isn't that everyone's fate? And, arguably, everyone's purpose?

And here's where Camus and Ishiguro agree. Through the acceptance of mortality and later through the act of dying, one proves one's authenticity. Even these clones; especially these clones. They die their own individual deaths the likes of which no one else has ever experienced or ever will. In Camus' world, and (so far) in ours, no two people are exactly alike. In Ishiguro's world, some people are exactly alike; when they're alive, the students are copies. But when they die, they are singular.

Death, especially his acceptance and invitation of it, is what makes Meursault Meursault. Death is what makes the clones in *Never Let Me Go* human, thereby serving a purpose arguably greater than the anatomical one they were created to fulfill. Somewhat paradoxically, the clones serve this purpose, fated though it is, while exercising free will. They not only accept their unseemly destinies, they voluntarily enact them.

My students keep asking why, if these kids know that their purpose and destiny is to donate organs to "normals" and then to die, they don't simply run away? Especially when they move away from school and there are no guardians—they can take hikes and trips and are even able to score a car every now then. Why do they come back? Why don't they seek new fortunes, new fates?

We come up with a few possible answers, the primary one being that the characters simply don't know what else to do. They aren't part of the real world and never have been; it's mythos to them. For fifteen years, they never passed beyond the Hailsham grounds, scared to death of the woods that surrounded them. They don't know where to go or how to begin changing their destinies.

We also figure that the clones don't run away because if they reject their fates and, thus, their purpose for existing in the first place, they also reject their identities. Although this rejection could be exhilarating in its liberation, the enormity of the void it would leave would be terrifying.

The clones accept their purpose, even when the grisly implications become clear. "'I was pretty much ready when I became a donor. It felt right. After all, it's what we're supposed to be doing, isn't it?'" Ruth says, entering into her destiny as though stepping into a long hallway with only one exit. All of these students, including Kathy and Tommy even as they pursue the deferral, embrace the fate they've been raised to fulfill.

"It's funny," Ishiguro says, fogging up his glasses and rubbing them with the end of his shirt, "that in this way, Tommy and Kathy and all the rest of them are like Meursault. They just roll with it." He puts his glasses back on and blinks rapidly.

Camus crosses his arms. "Meursault didn't believe in fate."

"Sure he did—death."

"*Bien sûr.*" Camus gestures impatiently. "The fate of all man is death. Meursault neither seeks nor avoids death; it does not enslave or rule him. It carries no meaning—it simply is."

"If Meursault had been raised at Hailsham, would he have accepted his fate as a donor without complaint or comment?" Ishiguro crosses his right foot onto his left knee and leans in.

"If Meursault had been raised at Hailsham, he would not be Meursault," Camus says.

* * *

Our explanations for why the clones never make a break for it don't do much to chip away at the book's grimy darkness. My students struggle to make sense of Ishiguro's intentions—is he suggesting that fate swallows free will? Is he advocating surrender?

"The book is about how we face the knowledge that our time on earth is limited and how we decide what things are the really worthwhile things," Ishiguro said at a conference in Liverpool in 2007. If trying to escape their brutal, early deaths isn't "worthwhile," what is?

One possible answer is something both Ishiguro and Camus advocate, albeit in fairly disparate manifestations—individuality. My students understood the connection between individuality and free will when we read *The Stranger* and they sense this connection more deeply now. They see and feel how it pertains to their own lives because *Never Let Me Go* widens the gap between "normal" and "other," between who we were born to be and who we want to be.

Kathy, Tommy, Ruth and all the other clones are literal copies—they're not physiological or genetic individuals, and they've all been reared since infancy in the same environment. Their demonstrations of free will involve recognizing and distinguishing themselves and each other as individuals. They do this by cultivating emotional and idiosyncratic personalities—Tommy has his temper tantrums, Ruth dominates others and wants to know everything, Kathy pans through her memories like a desperate gold rusher, driven by nostalgia and the nagging feeling that there's something she still hasn't quite pieced together.

"But all the feelings are such clichés!" Camus says. "'Oh, I'm so upset. Oh, I'm so confused. Oh, I feel so bad about what I said…' It's a silly performance in a show so old it's rotten."

I'm inclined to ask Albert to ease up a little, but I'm afraid he'll kick me in the cerebellum with his taper-toed boot.

Camus tucks a cigarette behind his ear. "You don't need emotions to be an individual. Look at Meursault—his lack of emotion is a defining element of his individuality. The rest is what Meursault does or doesn't do. He demonstrates nonconformity with action or inaction, rather than with emotion."

Ishiguro rubs his moustache, smoothes it back down. "But actions come from somewhere, right? They're a result of thoughts, beliefs and feelings. The characters in my book all receive the same practical, moral and experiential education, so thoughts and beliefs don't really distinguish them from one another. If they're going to come into their own, they have to start on the inside."

"Then distinguish thoughts and beliefs from the emotional quicksand." Camus lowers his voice to a stage whisper. "And from sentimental storytelling, while you're at it." He clears his throat. "Do we really want to pull at our feelings like errant threads? What's that going to do for us? For your clones?"

"Perhaps their time would be better spent exploring religion?" Ishiguro asks.

Camus laughs from the belly. "One thing I like about your book, Ishi, is that these kids never go there. There is no God. There's only us, from beginning to end."

When Kathy and Tommy don't rebel after learning that the deferral is just a rumor, when they submit to fate, my students feel that Tommy and Kathy have failed somehow. But the pursuit of the deferral is about something more than squeezing a few more years out of their short lives—it's about proving their humanity to a world that regards them, if at all, as something less than human.

"'We took away your art because we thought it would reveal your souls. Or to put it more finely, we did it to *prove you had souls at all*...it's still not a notion universally held,'" their teacher, Miss Emily, tells them after she debunks the rumor of the deferral. The nonexistence of the deferral reinforces the tightening coils of the clones' mortality, and reminds us that although the clones aren't born, they leave the world the same way as the rest of us. Mortality itself doesn't make the clones human, but their pursuit of the deferral despite its improbability does.

The clones, particularly Tommy and Kathy, transcend what they and the "normals" perceive as their limits—not intellectual, professional, or geographical limits, but emotional ones. The clones are created for their healthy human organs, yet the greatest proof of their humanity lies in their emotional range and experience. Ishiguro affirms that feeling anything passionately is worthwhile regardless of the outcome. He makes the argument in favor of heartbreak, a strictly human phenomenon, and an experience which would further intensify the interplay between the book and my personal life.

Just before we read *Never Let Me Go*, I fell head over heels for a guy. Thoughts of him seeped into my most mundane routines, into the books I was reading, and into the classroom, thrumming through me, delivering jolts to a mechanism that hadn't run in ages. When the relationship fell apart a few weeks later, I was devastated. I couldn't imagine days being only what they had been before this current ran through them.

My friend Jamie connected the dots when I called her, bereft over the loss of that brief luminescence. She said, "I know you're sad and I'm sad for you. But during the last few weeks there's been a quality to your voice and your laugh that I haven't heard in so long. Since before your dad died. Since you thought the chemo was working. Since you believed that he might be okay. It's been wonderful to hear you like that, excited, full of anticipation. This isn't about some guy or even about love—this is about hope."

The difference between my life over the past few weeks and my life over the past couple years is, simply, hope. I've decided I don't want to live without it. For me, a state of hopefulness is a state of happiness. And if hopefulness is a conscious choice, then so is happiness.

The desire to hope brings with it an instant pre-hopefulness, like feeling better 10 seconds after taking medicine. When I experience it, I realize that despite never actually choosing to be pessimistic, I have often chosen not to hope. After Dad died, the letting go of hope was automatic. I desired only preoccupation, sleep, and any other reprieve from the creeping hollowness I felt.

It's far easier said than done, but here it is: one can choose to *want* to be hopeful despite the knowledge that one's hope probably won't be realized. This is free will. This is bravery.

This is why hope in *Never Let Me Go* is so important, regardless of whether it's "false." The most important choice Kathy and Tommy make isn't to pursue the deferral or to accept their fate—it's to hope.

"They're hoping to stave off death," Camus says. "Granted, it's only for a little while, but still—that's not acceptance. Even Tommy, a guy who's missing half his vital organs, tries to eke out a few more years. What's the sense in that?" He lights a cigarette and holds his palm over the still-lit match.

"It's not what you hope for that matters." Ishiguro drums the backs of his heels against my shoulder.

"What about when Tommy's minutes from his fourth donation, hoping that he'll 'complete'? It's like Meursault being forced to hope that the guillotine will work the first time. At some point, reality and hope collide and reality is left standing. Or, as you know all too well from Nagasaki, perhaps not much is left standing. In any case, the moment is what exists." Camus blows out the match, sending the smell of sulfur into the air.

"The choice always exists," Ishiguro says, his voice rising like the moon behind my shoulder.

They're both right: the moment always exists, but inherent in the moment—if we want it to be—is choice. We can choose to do or feel nothing, and perhaps sometimes that's best. But we can choose something over nothing. Tommy and Kathy choose to wish on Ruth's slip of paper as though it's a star, not a satellite. They exercise free will by consciously choosing against the odds, by saying hey, we don't care what's likely to happen, we don't care if we have destinies, we don't care if we're going to die. We still choose hope. And if they can do it, so can I.

* * *

This is the class that, all throughout *The Stranger*, pulled for Meursault, cheered his potential and hoped that he would change—at least enough to save himself. This is the class that, after initially thinking that Meursault's freewheeling attitude was pretty awesome, rejected it because of its incompatibility with hope. And now here we are, tangling with the question of whether hope is valuable enough to overcome a particularly grisly reality.

I look at what I've written on the board, the two possibilities. It's like setting up an algebra equation incorrectly—it's impossible to solve, not because you're incapable of figuring out the answer, but because you haven't properly defined the problem.

"Maybe it doesn't matter whether your hope is realized or not. It's not about the outcome. It's about the act of hoping," I say to them. "Hope itself is the reason, is itself the goal." I half expect the bells ringing in me to resonate through the classroom and through them, but all that echoes is the same static that accompanies most other pauses and transitions.

Sam Connell's eyes are big behind his glasses and he nods almost imperceptibly. Some of them agree, some of them don't, and some of them don't care one way or another. They're free to find meaning where I do, or not, or somewhere else, or nowhere at all, yet I find myself thinking that they don't really get how fundamental this is. How perfectly obvious, yet nearly invisible in its obviousness. I wish someone had told me, an impossibly jaded teenager, that this was true. But had that happened and had I—improbably— understood, I wouldn't be having this moment now, teetering like my students on the verge of the jagged, messy hills of free will and feeling below me not emptiness or fear, but a space full of possibility.

"You know, I read *The Stranger* in high school," Ishiguro says. "Not for class—on my own."

"Of course," Camus says. "And?" He extends his pack of smokes.

"I never smoke, but what the hell," Ishiguro says, taking a cigarette. "I read it on the beach in one afternoon. Sunburned my back, too—I don't think I moved a muscle from cover to cover. I read the last line over and over instead of going in the water. 'For me to feel less alone, I had only to wish that there be a large crowd of spectators the day of my execution and that they greet me with cries of hate.'" Ishiguro shakes his head appreciatively. "I remember thinking that I could die happy if I'd written that line."

Camus smiles and leans across my collarbone to light Ishiguro's cigarette. "Die happy. A fine choice."

Ishiguro shrugs and takes a drag. "I guess Meursault and I have something in common after all." Smoke trails from his mouth as he speaks. "Life is a funny old dog sometimes." He coughs over his shoulder and takes another drag.

"That it is," Camus says. "And you can't teach an old dog new tricks."

Ishiguro exhales, copying Camus' gesture perfectly. "That's why the first thing you teach a puppy is that learning new tricks is possible," Ishiguro says.

The bell rings. Teenagers rush past me into the hallway, into the world, to make of it what they will, what they can. I'm seized by their humanity, the scuff of their sneakers on the floor, the impatient cadence of their conversations, their faces emerging from the hoods of their sweatshirts. The blazing whites of their wide eyes.

Finding Fathers

On one of the countless nights I spent in my dad's arms looking over his shoulder at the vast landscape of his political paraphernalia, I said my first word: "button." The senators, representatives and presidents, who I imagined kept donkeys and elephants as pets, were like friends who smiled and waved at me. After a disastrous cropped haircut, my mom stitched "I am a girl" on the front of a tight orange cap before sending me off to preschool, but she had to do no such thing to remind me of my political affiliation. I called the mean kids at school gerrymanderers.

My dad taught political science for 37 years and wrote constitutional law textbooks. Before I was born, he served as the County Commissioner of my hometown. For over 10 years he managed the campaign of Mary Brown, our local state representative. He was a different sort of politician, if you could call him a politician. He was a different sort of man.

When my dad discussed politics, he'd set down his

pen or fork or papers and his hands would join the conversation, rolling over terrain the way a mountain goat navigates a craggy hillside. He'd explain and weigh and listen, and he'd always find a way to give the political process the benefit of the doubt. The purity with which he loved the experiment of politics, even when it exploded and made a mess, made me believe him. I used to tell him he should run for president. The older I got, the more serious I became about this—I don't know anyone who wouldn't have voted for my dad and for the tangible and mighty force of his goodwill.

He had an uncanny ability to predict politics—the nature of an October surprise, who'd be elected and by how much, which platforms would be compelling to whom. He kept an elaborate spreadsheet of local and state races and used his own system to calculate each candidate's odds of winning, buying and trading buttons accordingly. He gave interviews on local television and radio stations every election season.

Election Day used to be a holiday for me. Like other children anticipated slumber parties and birthdays, I counted down to the first Tuesday in November. On election nights, my dad would take me to Mary Brown's house, where graph paper covered the walls like giant crossword puzzles, precincts named and numbered, percentages scrawled in a politician's hiero-glyphics. I'd sit at the top of the stairs and watch people fill in numbers, answer phones, rush about. The whole scene crackled, especially if there was a presidential race underway (George Bush's succession of Reagan didn't dampen our spirits due to complete lack of surprise; Clinton's defeat of Bush led to the kind of exhausted partying that I'd heard happened in college after finals). Mary Brown's elections were every two years, and she never lost.

After midnight I'd hear the clapping, my dad would hoist me onto his shoulders and I'd shake hands as if I were the new President. Dad and I wouldn't leave until late; I learned I could fall asleep standing up if I leaned against something. The numbers on the dashboard were almost unrecognizable, shocking and brazen in their glowing announcement that we were closing in on 3 a.m. He'd let me stay home from school the next day; we'd watch game shows and eat *Grape Nuts*.

I was in a campaign ad with Mary Brown when I was seven. We walked in Milham Park and fed bread to the ducks while a calm voice narrated her policies. Once, during the annual Doo Dah Parade, Mary Brown rode a donkey and waved at the crowd while Dad, clad in a pair of overalls with a patch over the seat, walked behind her, shoveling the mess into a burlap bag. I think he enjoyed shucking his khakis for farmer gear as much as we enjoyed seeing him that way. He wasn't above getting his hands dirty, wasn't above any job with a purpose.

When I turned 16, I got two jobs—one at a donut mill and the other working for the Kalamazoo Democratic Party. I canvassed for the man who succeeded Mary Brown as state representative, as well as for the Democratic gubernatorial candidate. I wanted to contribute to the system my dad had spent his life studying and helping to power, to expand my link to him into something adult and important.

I wanted my involvement in the process to be meaningful, but I was still a kid. One night while driving with some friends, I noticed a neighborhood full of Republican yard signs. I yelled at the owners from inside the car, pointing out the weak spots in the Republican policies and extolling the virtues of the Democratic candidates. My friends got caught up in the moment—they believed what I believed, just as I believed what my dad believed—and we decided we needed to make a statement. We thought we could do something important and for the greater good while demonstrating the passionate rebellion of the '60s that our parents still celebrated. We drove to a supermarket, bought black spray paint, and defaced the yard signs. The police who caught us were perplexed—they'd never before apprehended vandals bent only on making political statements. My friends left me to explain our actions to the police and to our parents.

My dad, typically not one to permit illegality or irresponsibility, listened to my explanation and apology, and after I promised never to do it again and to respect other people's opinions, as wrong as they might seem, he hugged me and whispered in my ear that he was proud. He sensed political adrenaline and recognized that we were banging on the door of a process we had only begun to understand. He knew that the important thing was that we were moved.

My dad was a politician from a generation that revered the president. When he was a teenager, people lined up along the boulevard to wave at Eisenhower's motorcade, thrilled simply to be that close to power and greatness. He spoke of those days with nostalgia, which I grabbed hold of when George W. Bush was elected and, for so many of us, the U.S. presidency became something of a joke.

In 2000, I was living in Ireland. I went to sleep at 7 a.m. after the networks pronounced Al Gore victorious. I thought I was still dreaming when I awoke a

Joelle Renstrom

few hours later to a red map and a picture of Bush's grinning face. Like everyone else, I couldn't figure out what had happened or how or why. Dad went on TV and radio stations to provide insight and explanations, to try and predict what would happen now. The interviewers weren't looking for prognostication—I think they just wanted him to say that he hadn't lost faith in the system, that it wouldn't fall apart.

Across the pond, I was accosted by anyone who discerned that I was American. Shopkeepers, waitresses, mailmen, people on the DART demanded to know what had happened and why. "What's wrong with you?" some of them asked. I didn't answer. I couldn't. I didn't know. I'd mumble feeble excuses about how I'd voted absentee for Gore and I'd apologize and stumble away. The more I travelled, the more confusion and anger I encountered, from the anti-American graffiti in Budapest bathroom stalls to the articles in European magazines. When some Canadians I travelled with gave me some maple leaf pins, I wore them and let foreigners assume I was Canadian.

I sent my dad lengthy emails describing the situations I encountered. I wanted him to tell me that everything was going to be okay, that Bush's questionable election didn't mean that America had crossed a point of no return. Instead of being upset, Dad was curious about how the process would play out. We're a relatively young country, he said. We need to make mistakes, we need to be confused, and we need to test the system and see it triumph and reset its course.

Four years later I watched from Canada as we kept Bush in office. The vitriol I experienced from Canadians dwarfed that from Europeans. Canadians generally accept, though resentfully, the "trickle-up effect"—whatever happens in the U.S. eventually seeps north across the border. Some Canadians argue that they should be able to vote for our president, since it directly affects them. The comments in the weeks after the election permeated classrooms, lunchrooms, CBC broadcasts, bus station vestibules. Four years earlier, I'd been able to tell myself that Europeans didn't hate Americans—they resented our government and politics. But when we reelected Bush, we could no longer argue that our administration wasn't an extension of us as people. We'd kept ourselves in the mess; we'd invited the wrath.

I felt as if I'd swallowed a cannonball. I called my dad. "How can you have faith in this system?" I asked him. Last time was bad enough, but this? Didn't he feel as though the entire system had up and slapped him in the face? How could he create meaning from his life's work given the blatant disregard for the values he held dear?

When I finished, he chuckled and said, "You're far too young to be so jaded."

"Aren't you?" I asked him.

"Nah," he said, as though the landscape was still easy to navigate. I had expected him to admit that he was putting his political beliefs on the table for reexamination, but he didn't. He told me that politics moves like the economy—it ebbs and flows, spikes and plummets and cycles around and around. He admitted that yes, this was a low point, but that as with most nadirs, it would usher in something amazing.

Had this response come from anyone else, I might have dismissed it as Pollyannaism. But because it came from him, I listened. And deep down where I wasn't terrified to hope, I believed him.

Despite the frustration and sadness, there was a political bright spot in 2004. We both watched the Democratic National Convention and I said to him, "How about that Obama guy?" When I asked where he was from, what his story was, my dad told me. He had all of Obama's senatorial campaign buttons and had been following his trajectory since 1997. He also had some idea where Obama was going. "Keep your eye on that fellow," he said to me.

* * *

I pulled *Dreams from My Father* off my dad's bookshelf the summer before the 2008 election, just before I moved from Kalamazoo to Boston. It had been two years since I'd moved back to my hometown, trying to fill—or at least not feel utterly consumed by—the gaping hole where my dad used to be. I read the book knowing that I would soon put distance between me and the rest of the family, this town and its familiar hospitals, and in some ways, the man I am still looking for. I read most of the book in my old bedroom in the untried silence of late afternoon, leaning back in the big gold chair with my feet propped on the desk, in his old stance.

Dreams from My Father is not a political rags to riches story; it's the story of humanity unfolding. Most politicians don't stop to take spiritual journeys— they don't have time, or they think it's for pansies or it never occurs to them. They don't cultivate much beyond business acumen, shrewd political strategies, and networking skills. They don't do walkabouts.

This is why *Dreams from My Father* resonates so deeply with me. Obama's journey has at times been sloppy and painful, and movement has not always been forward. He unapologetically recalls being a kid, a teenager who sometimes did well in school and sometimes didn't, and then a college student who got drunk and smoked pot and tried blow. Obama doesn't hide from any iteration of himself, nor does he hide from us. We've all looked in some unlikely and unproductive places as we groped in the dark for a light switch, a foothold, anything that might orient us and make sense of the world. Like my dad, he knows how necessary it is to ask who and what we are, what we believe, what part we play in it all; he knows that we can't pursue the answers without pushing limits and, sometimes, screwing up. Obama's trajectory as a politician and a person is neither linear nor simple— like a winding river, it splits into tributaries that continue to veer and grow and then, somehow, wind back around and meet back up again, forces joining.

Reading about Obama's fearless self-exploration and the subsequent payoffs confirmed my belief that the search for answers is endless and often messy, and that in many ways, the search itself is the answer. His story filled me with a renewed sense of confidence and purpose at a time of consuming anticipation and anxiety, when I stood below humid clouds that presage a thunderclap, preparing to start my life again. For the first time since Dad died, I found myself thinking that maybe I'd come out of this okay after all. Maybe more than okay. Although it wasn't fully reintegrated into my life or my lexicon just yet, I could conceive of hope.

* * *

On Tuesday, November 4, 2008, the story of my father kicked up like a breeze, gently at first, and then more insistent, rustling my insides, making noise.

I went to a returns party with some colleagues. Everyone ate cheese and crackers and drank wine with confident conviviality as the electoral count grew more and more promising—Pennsylvania turned blue, then Virginia. Phones buzzed nonstop as people flitted around, circling the furniture like they were playing a high stakes game of musical chairs. My palms sweat and my heart swung wildly in my chest. I was more invested in the election than I had been in anything since Dad got sick; it was far too late to prevent myself from hoping. I left before the official announcement because I had to be alone when it came.

I went home, turned on CNN, and sat on the edge

of the couch, bathed in the glow of cathode rays. Ohio turned blue. Wolf Blitzer stopped talking to holograms and called it. Something opened inside me and I cried like a dam bursting.

I rode my bike to the Boston Commons, to what felt like a city-wide birthday party. People danced under the streetlights, swinging each other around as though they were in a musical—unfettered and unabashed, radiant. The triumph was so thick I could curl my hands around it and hang on tight. Some of my students danced in the fray. Senator John Kerry rode by and yelled from the window, "Barack wants you to be responsible and safe!" and the kids cheered—they'd do anything Obama said.

Old, young, black, white, homeless, rich—all equalized that night. All the stories Obama found as he visited families and congregations, all those woes he sought out because they presented something tangible to soothe, gathered up to dance with other people's stories, all the histories brewing up one big storm. For a night, rapture removed people from their struggles and guilts and regrets and replaced them with movement and hope.

I tried to summon my dad. I closed my eyes and cleared my mind to make space for a response—James Taylor playing on a passing car radio, a shooting star, that feeling of him right behind me. I tipped my head to the sky and asked, "Are you watching this?"

Obama knows what it means to search, both in the world and inside himself, for a lost father. He knows what it means to be defined by someone's absence. My father was more of a presence for me than Obama's was for him; my dad helped me search for answers, whereas his was the source of many of the questions that prompted searching. Still, both of our fathers made us want to look, and looking is what gives us stories to tell.

The night Obama was elected president, I overturned 30 years of personal philosophy by choosing to believe that not only was my dad still around somehow, but that he knew what was happening. I decided to believe that he was doing the afterlife equivalent of drinking a beer, eating popcorn and watching this thing unfold. Perhaps Obama imagines his doing the same, cheering dreams like race horses, applauding when they cross the line.

Closing the Book

I've been on the same page of Gabriel García Márquez's *Love in a Time of Cholera* for 47 months.

I started it in 2006, when I first moved back to Kalamazoo, Michigan. The book has lived on my nightstand ever since, its red and black hardcover at first shiny, then dusty, now grimy, covered with film.

Love in a Time of Cholera is the book I was reading when Dad died. It was the book I brought to his chemotherapy treatments every Wednesday.

I actually looked forward to Wednesdays because they meant eight hours of hanging out with him. I'd pack him a lunch, something simple like a turkey sandwich on soft wheat bread with lettuce, melon or a pear, sometimes Jell-O or pudding. It was like packing a child's lunch; nothing spicy or hot or cold or acidic or lumpy or sharp. I'd bring Dad's MP3 player, onto which I'd uploaded playlists—Motown, happy, my favorites, angry, funky, sad. I'd bring a spare oxygen tank. Once, at a four-way stop downtown, I braked suddenly and the tank crashed against a lawn chair in the back. The spigot unleashed a violent hiss that made me think the car was going to explode, as though a bomb had been tossed through the window. Then I remembered that what was leaking out of the canister wouldn't kill me and I pulled over and twisted the valve shut. I'd bring newspapers. Drinks. Pillows. Like packing for a day at the beach.

We'd sit in adjacent Lay-Z-Boys. Dad would recline next to me as toxic chemicals pumped from the complicated IV system next to him, a jellyfish hanging from a tree, two tentacles hooked up to his port, cancer-fighting drugs and alternating bags of saline and anti-nausea medicine. The port scared me. It seemed like something out of the *Twilight Zone*—a small silver circle shaped like a screw nut, visible under the skin, from which a catheter ran, connecting the port to a central vein for maximum bloodstream efficiency. Sometimes they attach the port to the jugular; I didn't think to ask which vein they chose on my dad. If I put my head on his chest, I felt something hard, unbeating, and I'd get very scared.

We'd read. Sometimes we'd doze. Sometimes we'd talk to other patients. We often listened to the MP3 player with a headphone splitter, the music travelling to us via the same lines, arriving at the same time into the ports of our ears. Sometimes we'd lie there awake with our eyes closed, thinking, worrying, wishing.

We did this every Wednesday. I arranged my teaching schedule to keep Wednesdays open. The week after he died, a message popped up on Wednesday morning. Reminder: hang out with Dad.

* * *

Four years later, I pick up *Love in a Time of Cholera* again. It feels like a promise I never kept, something unfinished from a different time, a different life. It won't stop haunting my bedside table until I've read it.

The book opens with Dr. Juvenal Urbino, the most revered man in the town, tending to the death of his close friend. I curl up and lean in, looking for words to grip me with their weight, their profundity in relation to my dad's death or to the four years since then. Dr. Urbino believes "'[e]ach man is the master of his own death, and all that we can do when the time comes is to help him die without fear of pain.'" My eye settles jerkily on that line, like a needle skipping on a record. A sense of disquiet moves from behind my eyelids down into my stomach. I close the book and stare at its cover, trying to remember what it was like to read the book the first time. I try to remember why I chose to start reading *Love in a Time of Cholera* then. It had to mean something—how does one coincidentally immerse herself in a book about love and sickness and death as the person she loves most dozes, slowly dying, beside her?

I consider putting the book back on the nightstand. But there are only two weeks until the semester starts; if I don't read it now, it'll be at least another nine months before I consider reading it again. Maybe it'll be another four years.

The anniversary of Dad's death is only a couple of weeks away. Four years ago, I had just moved back to Kalamazoo. Four years ago we were studying treatment protocols, organizing the medicine cabinet, creating spreadsheets. Four years ago I slept with the phone next to my pillow, waking up once or twice just to make sure it was on, that I hadn't missed a call.

My body is as conscious of the date of his death as my mind—in fact, my body usually remembers first. My muscles contract into hard little balls and I wake up in the middle of the night with charley horses. All the time I feel vaguely nauseated, as though the remnants of something old and dirty sit in my stomach. It's coming, my body says silently in a million idiosyncratic ways. The day of his passing.

* * *

Four years ago, the oncologist enrolled Dad in a clinical trial, explaining that Dad would receive conventional chemotherapy no matter what, and that through the clinical trial he'd either get a placebo or a cocktail of experimental drugs. We crossed our fingers and Dad landed in the second group which, according to the oncologist, was "very good news." He said that Dad likely had only six months left, but if the clinical trial was successful, he might live for a couple of years. A couple of years could stretch to five years, we thought. 5 years could be 10.

The chemo was awful. Dad couldn't eat anything spicy or acidic because of the sores on his lips and in his mouth. He couldn't eat anything hot or cold because extreme temperatures interacted badly with the chemo, resulting in numbness of the lips, mouth, and throat. Almost any food smell provoked nausea. Altogether, he lost nearly 80 pounds. When I put my arms around him, they met over his spine.

As my dad dozed in the recliner, I'd watch him

closely and try to measure the depth and frequency of his breaths. As the weeks passed, he seemed to be breathing better, his chest less concave, his cheeks tinged with pink. I was afraid of his death, of course, but for a few short weeks, death had been relegated to an abstraction that would someday, though not any day soon, become real.

A few weeks after Dad started chemotherapy, a CT scan revealed a 50% reduction of cancer cells in his lungs and liver. He stopped carrying around an oxygen tank, able to breathe on his own; he started eating foods other than applesauce and cantaloupe. "This could actually turn out okay," said the oncologist.

The act of reading *Love in a Time of Cholera* was, like almost everything else immediately following Dad's CT scan, hopeful. I luxuriated in the lushness of García Márquez's prose, drinking it in, letting it counteract the smell of chemicals in the oncologist's office. The last time I picked up the book was during Dad's last chemotherapy session, about two weeks before he died. The bookmark, the gold ribbon attached to the spine, is still there. Page 132. Last time I was on this page, he was still alive. No one thought that his last session of chemotherapy would be the Wednesday I finished page 131; no one had any idea that the cancer was quietly putting into motion a new and insidious plan. The person who stopped on this page at 4 p.m. on a Wednesday afternoon in late August didn't know anything.

* * *

This time, the act of reading the book is fraught with tension. I look at my fingers' hard grip on the edges of the book and the veins standing out on my hands. Reading this book is no longer a luxury.

As I read *Love in a Time of Cholera* and get nearer to the bookmark, I think back four years, but not because anything particular in the text prompts me to do so. Sure, I could try to plumb meaning out of this book that applies to Dad's death, or to the last four years recovering from it—there's a ravaging disease involved, and the protagonist of the novel watches her husband die—but I don't think about any of that because I can never quite forget that this was the book I was reading when he died. As I read, I feel almost suffocated by the love between Fermina Daza and Florentino Ariza. As I draw nearer to the gold ribbon, I find myself coming up empty when I search for meaningful symbolism. But I read on, though sometimes I catch myself merely scanning the lines, and then, ashamed, I flip back a couple pages and start again.

About 10 pages too soon, I flip to page 132 and lift the ribbon from the crease:

"His obsession was the dangerous lack of sanitation in the city. He appealed to the highest authorities to fill in the Spanish sewers…He was aware of the mortal threat of the drinking water. The mere idea of building an aqueduct seemed fantastic…."

I smile. This is perfect—utterly devoid of symbolism or emotion.

After a minute, I wonder which of the male characters the passage is referring to, since it doesn't particularly sound like anyone in the book. I turn back a page. Juvenal Urbino has just returned to his old family home, which has been empty since his father's death from cholera six years earlier; he is referring to his father. After a sleepless night, Urbino takes residence in his father's old office, examining and exploring all the relics left there. I turn back to 132. In his father's office, Urbino finds wooden water collectors that dripped rainwater into jars: "But Dr. Juvenal Urbino was not taken in by these appearances of purity, for he knew that despite all precautions, the bottom of each earthen jar was a sanctuary for waterworms. He had spent the slow hours of his childhood watching them with an almost mythical astonishment…." I can't blink away the image of a little kid looking into his dad's jars and seeing these worms, as though the kid could see right into the depths of his father, into all things flawed and wonderful, where parasites became magical.

I don't remember whether I read that passage the first time or not—I don't remember anything about Urbino's father or their relationship from my first foray into the story. It's a relatively small detail in a book that focuses primarily on another relationship, but it's the detail that creates a link between the text and me—a connection between 4 years ago and now.

Two weeks after Dad's positive CT scan, he went into the hospital with his second bowel obstruction in a month. When they X-rayed him they noticed his lungs suddenly looked much worse. In 10 days, the cancer had not only stopped shrinking, but had reversed course and flourished, especially in his lungs. The oncologist said that in 20 years of practice, he'd never seen colon cancer behave like this. All throughout, we'd been told things like, "there's only a very slim chance it's spread to the lungs," and so on. We were fed odds when no real prognosis or explanation existed; we were patted on the back and offered a series of almost-promises as compensation for all the unforeseen setbacks and the way Dad managed to get into that tiny minority on everything.

Love in a Time of Cholera stayed in the chemo bag for the eight days he was in the hospital that last time. I didn't think about it once.

Initially, the doctors focused on removing the obstruction, but it became clear that the cancer in the lungs was a much more serious issue and that it probably didn't matter what was happening in his colon. On regular rotation were his oncologist, a surgeon, a hospitalist, an internist, a respiratory therapist, a gastroenterologist, and at least three nurses. In a hospital, you start over all the time, with each face. You have to remember when you talked to whom and what was said, not just to get what you need, but to remind yourself that you're not crazy. We kept a file on a laptop and logged every diagnostic and treatment-related conversation we had. We had the same conversations over and over, asking repeatedly for the same things, appealing to different people for another blanket, more morphine, for some other option, some window of possibility.

Now, as the act of reading *Love in a Time of Cholera* catalyzes these memories, I feel as though I'm remembering a horrible movie I once saw. Maybe I'm preventing myself from fully accessing those moments, making sure I stay outside them. I have flashes of remembering how very real those moments are. Yet a few minutes later I read over the words curiously, thinking, oh yeah, that's right—that happened. Even though I lived it, I still cannot fathom this happening. All I know is that I wouldn't go through it again for anything.

* * *

During those eight days, I left the hospital only a couple times to shower and to get things from my apartment. I slept in Dad's room, usually on a chair next to the bed, bent at the waist, arms folded under my head, resting next to him. I kept thinking something would go horribly wrong if I left, that somehow disaster was less likely if I was keeping watch.

During those last eight days, he had a paradoxical reaction to the sedative Ativan and hallucinated for over a day. He picked at the blankets, pulling pills of fabric, worrying them with his fingers. At one point, he seemed to be hammering something, maybe building a shelf. Many of his hallucinations involved food. In a daze, he would cut pieces from what he probably imagined was prime rib, or maybe salmon. He'd reach his hand up, lifting slowly, as though the

Joelle Renstrom

bite might fall off, his mouth searching for the fork. He'd open his mouth and take the bite softly, as though biting the bud of a flower. How much he must have missed food, missed the tastes that didn't turn to metal in his mouth, missed the days when his stomach didn't revolt against itself.

After they put the gastric tube in, he couldn't eat anything. Done with the chemo that made him unable to drink or eat anything hot or cold or acidic or spicy, he told me he was going out to get ice cream. I asked him what flavors sounded good. Root beer float, he said. That's what I'd get.

The man deserved one last root beer float. He deserved a lot more than that. But over the past four years, I've thought a lot about that float.

I also think about that time near the end when I ate a pear in front of him. That looks good, he said. Can I have one? He grinned at me like a little boy. I had to tell him that no, he couldn't have one. That's okay, he said, so patient now upon his dying, unfazed by his unrequited desire for the pear. Every time I bite into the grainy softness of a Bartlett I think about how he will never eat another pear, about how at the end we should have been able to give him something that tasted good.

At the end, his lungs under siege, he started having episodes of being unable to breathe, which triggered panic attacks. His eyes opened wide, tearing at the corners, his hands grasping at nothing, at anything, trying to get air. One night he had a panic attack every 45 minutes. My brother, sister, and I stayed up with him. We held his hands and looked straight into his terrified face and told him to keep his eyes open and focus on us. We inhaled deeply and slowly with him, coached him. Not unlike Lamaze, probably. Breathing lessons.

Just as he helped bring me into the world, I helped him leave.

The oncologist told us the latest CT scan showed his lungs were overrun with cancer. There was nothing left to do. This news triggered another panic attack, and while my brother talked Dad through it, the oncologist pulled me into the hallway and told me he thought Dad was terrified and hadn't made peace with his own mortality. Fuck you, I wanted to say. Who has?

There were a couple of last ditch efforts—treating his lungs for possible complicating pneumonia, sending the surgeon back in to discuss what we all knew wasn't even a viable possibility of somehow routing Dad's intestines around the blockage. But by then we all knew the score.

The oncologist said he'd come by again the next day. He called instead. I answered the phone and became the custodian of this information: that the clinical trial had officially failed, that he'd "called it in." He wasn't even going to stop by—it was that over. I needed to ask him questions. What was actually going to happen when he died? What would it be like? What were we supposed to do? I repeated the phrase "what will it look like?" until he told me that as his organs started shutting down, Dad would go comatose. Colon, liver, kidneys, heart, one after the other.

I hung up and turned to face my family. They knew. "He says to keep on doing what we're doing," I said.

Dad's brother flew in from St. Paul. The last night Dad was conscious, we brought old childhood toys, artifacts, and pictures and we told stories. I admitted to taking his car out for joyrides when I was 15 and even to letting my little sister sit on my lap and steer. There were certain memories that were really accessible for him—watching a game seven Stanley Cup playoff game with my brother and me, leaving a note on Mom's windshield asking for a date, finally liberating my adopted sister from her Ukrainian orphanage. He told us what he wanted to tell us, what he loved most about us. I told him I'd dedicate my first book to him. He squeezed my hand and said, "that's great, but you have to finish it first." He had my number until the very end.

We told him what we thought death was and where we thought he'd be going. We acknowledged that death might simply be nothing, but we agreed that if that was indeed the case, there was no reason to freak out, because there was literally nothing to worry about. My uncle, a Methodist minister, talked about heaven—not in a lofty way, not in a harps and angels way, but as a rather practical place where people exist in a state of fulfillment. My brother talked about a spiritual return to nature. I talked about collective consciousness. My sister said she didn't know—she wasn't sure if she believed in God anymore, so she wasn't sure about heaven. Who knows, she said, maybe reincarnation. My dad was the only one who didn't have an idea about death. He couldn't picture it, couldn't sharpen it from blurry abstraction. We wanted to fill the abyss we were afraid he imagined. We needed to do something, because we couldn't stop the dying.

I asked one of the nurses how I'd know death was imminent so I could make sure everyone was there.

She told me to check his hands and feet—if they were cold, it meant his circulatory system was shutting down. His breathing would become shallow and the time between breaths would increase. I watched for these signs, trying not to seem obvious.

His breathing episodes became more frequent and intense. The doctors increased his morphine and added some Valium, which kept him resting peacefully. We said our goodbyes during one of his last bouts of consciousness. That night, he sat up gasping, eyes fixed on something far in the distance and we thought that was it. We stood around him and we each gave him permission to go, urged him to rest in peace. But that wasn't it. He slipped into a coma, breathing with the help of an oxygen mask.

We decided that he wouldn't be too thrilled with all of us being there, trying to sleep on the cold hard floor, so tired we could barely walk, getting further and further behind in work and in our own lives, so everyone else went home for a while. I asked the nurses to check his vitals every two hours so I'd have some idea when death was getting close. His heart was still pumping away, though, and his blood pressure remained steady. Even after three months of chemo, even after losing a third of his body weight, even on the brink of death, he was so strong—

especially his heart, which came as no surprise. I spent the last day alone with him, sitting in the small recliner the nurses brought us when they found out we were sleeping there. I played his favorite music— James Taylor, Tori Amos, Al Green. I talked to him, held his hands, told him I loved him, told him that I would take care of everyone, that he should let go.

* * *

On September 4, 2010, the fourth anniversary of his death, I take *Love in a Time of Cholera* to Mount Auburn Cemetery in Cambridge to finish the last 20 pages. I wander around until, on a small path, I see a weeping beech tree whose branches spread down like a leafy umbrella. I sit under the branches, the cool air sifting through the leaves, the sound of a dozen tiny fans fluttering around me.

I have trouble focusing on the book. The two people who have been in agonizing, all-consuming, uncon-summated love for 50 years have married, but I can't tell if I should be happy for them or sad that it took them so long. I charge on, determined to finish the book here, in the most beautiful cemetery I've ever seen.

* * *

At 1:15 in the morning on September 4—Labor

Day, that year—Dad died. My brother and I were with him, holding his hands. He hovered on the brink of death for a long time. Bent over him as though to catch any vestiges of him that we could, we watched his chest rise and fall, slower and slower, and each time he exhaled we'd wait, longer and longer each time, to see if he'd inhale again. We had the nurse check his vitals every hour so we'd be able to call my mom and sister, but then, suddenly, he was gone. Even though he looked no different, it was clear his body was just a shell and whatever had inhabited it was gone. The nurses took his nose tube, catheter, and IVs out, and used Crisco to remove his wedding ring.

I called my mom and told her she should come down. I used my best neutral voice to avoid making her panic, but my lack of urgency told her everything. It took her an hour to get to the hospital—she got lost on the way, driving in circles around a neighborhood she'd known for 40 years.

Then we had to go home. We had to go back to our lives, we had to figure out how to be in the world, how to live after having been woven into the process of dying.

Two weeks later, as I cleaned out the bag I'd brought to chemo each week I found the book, which seemed to look at me innocently, suspecting nothing, waiting for me to resume reading. I put it on my nightstand.

* * *

As I remember Dad's death now, as I run the reel in my head, I remember how I wasn't sure I would survive it. People die of grief—at least, I'd heard stories that assert as much: all the times a grandfather has followed his beloved wife of 60 years into death by a matter of minutes. García Márquez writes about people who die of heartbreak all the time, whether it's caused by death or by the sudden departure of a lover or by the collapse of the family business. For a long time, I thought that might happen to me.

But here I am, alive, and finally finishing *Love in a Time of Cholera.*

I am distracted by birds, by the wind, by thoughts so mundane they're embarrassing—what to make for dinner, what to wear to the party next week. I scold myself, remind myself I'm here to do something else. I'm here to try and commune with a ghost, but I do that every day, all the time. I'm here today finishing this book because I want to be with him. More than anything, I want to channel and re-inhabit who I was then, so I can be as close to him as I was when he died.

But I don't feel much like that person. In fact, I'm so far removed from who I was four years ago that I feel strange and a bit guilty, yet also relieved and gratified that things are so different now. Sometimes it feels like a betrayal to acknowledge that his death didn't kill me, that my life is better than it was four years ago, better even than it was before he got sick. Four years ago I couldn't have known or believed that I could ever be happy again, that I could learn how to function in a world in which my dad was dead, much less enjoy it. But I know this now, and it changes everything.

I close the book and wander through the cemetery. I climb the hill to the tower and take the stairs to the top. Who knew cemeteries could be this lovely? People stop in front of gravestones, sit by the pond and watch the ducks, stroll up the paths marked with little white signs: Snowdrop Path, Hibiscus Path, Pilgrim Path. Some cars wind through the roads, people who drive straight to a particular grave, who can't or don't want to amble, whose grief is too acute for anything other than efficiency. I wonder how many of us lost someone on September 4. I wonder how different the others are now than they were when it happened. Regardless, we're all here now. And some of us will climb the tower and see birds dipping between the branches, maybe a hawk circling above, squirrels hoarding acorns, vines and trees and flowers reaching toward the sky. Some of us will see the way the sun cuts sideways through the leaves, picking up particles of dust and making them shimmer gold, rotating slowly through the afternoon as if to mimic the turning of the earth itself, as if to affirm that we're still turning with it.

The Stars Are Not For Man

> "All the earlier changes your race has known took countless ages. But this is a transformation of the mind, not of the body. By the standards of evolution, it will be cataclysmic... It has already begun."
> Arthur Clarke, *Childhood's End*

I huddled next to a space heater on the porch, a blanket around me like a cape, watching the snow pile up on the sills. It was 4 p.m., that dead time between night and day, dark enough to be much later. I could hear the snow falling, hear it spreading heavily over everything. It was as though 2008 had passed seamlessly into reality; the utter lack of change covered everything.

Time, time, time, I thought over and over, the word echoing in my head with each snowflake that dropped unhurried from the sky and landed on the window, stuck fast like this moment, like the next, and the next. *Time for something else.*

It had been a year and a half since Dad died, since I moved back to Kalamazoo. Eighteen months seemed like an arbitrary measure of time; I had been here forever—perhaps I had never left—and yet in some way I was not here at all. I hung in Kalamazoo like a cloud swollen and ripe, waiting. *It's time,* I told myself again, trying to shake free of the thickness that settled down around me, trying to free myself, even if only for a fall.

When I moved to Kalamazoo, I picked up a few classes at the University where my dad had taught for nearly 40 years. My office was down the hall from his. Every time I went into the Freidmann Building using Dad's special key that opened the door on the back dock, I instantly became six years old. The smell was exactly the same—the parchment musk of an aged university building, the metal of old desks and filing cabinets, the smell of years of sun on paper and boxes. The small square tiles of the floor, the browns and yellows of the Political Science Department were the same. I remembered looking at the cartoons on Dad's office door, especially the caricatures of Reagan looking like Dracula and George Bush Sr. looking like Frankenstein. I remembered thinking that my dad's door was definitely the coolest one in the whole department. Eighteen months ago, I peeled off the yellowed tape and put the cartoons on my door.

Twice a week I'd spend a couple hours or so cleaning

out his office. I was overwhelmed by how much of him was crammed into that small space. Forty years' worth of the currency of his daily life—the papers, files, articles, books, awards, photographs, small tools, electronics, extra shoes, napkins, plastic utensils, funny little knick knacks. I dumped file after file into the recycling bin, thinking about how he'd feel if he could see me jettisoning all the materials he'd spent a lifetime accumulating. I felt complicit in their sudden and utter irrelevance.

Everything I found fit perfectly with who I knew my dad to be—the tiny screwdrivers in the pencil drawer, the toothpaste, the aspirin mixed in with the Post Its and index cards, the shelf of maps, the letters and thank you cards from students and other faculty members. Sometimes I leaned back and stretched my elbows and hands over the arms of the chair, rocking back and forth, trying to channel him. There were times the air turned humid and thick and full, and I'd swear he was in there with me. I tried to inhabit his office for the both of us, hunting his fading scent as though I'd been bred for it. If I didn't do his work, if I didn't haunt his spaces, if I didn't read his handwriting every day, he would really be dead. As long as someone was there, as long as lights were on and the door was open, it could, for a second, be him.

Every time I was in either of our offices, his colleagues—now my colleagues—would pop in and talk about how great it was that I was continuing his legacy. Even though it was a huge compliment to be known as his daughter, it was nearly impossible to avoid focusing on his death and how it had become the center of my life. Every time I came to campus I thought about how I wouldn't be there if he hadn't died.

It was time for me to think about other things.

* * *

During the winter of 2008, I taught "The Evolution of Science Fiction," a class I'd pitched a few months earlier to the Honors College. I thought it would be fun to talk about some of my favorite books with other geeks; I imagined showing *Babylon 5* in class and getting into expansive philosophical discussions about robotics, the infinite universe, and what it means to be human. I put Arthur Clarke's *Childhood's End* on the syllabus for the science fiction class without consciously thinking about how the book, how even just the title, connected to my life. In the book, a mysterious alien race called the Overlords descends upon earth and quietly makes significant societal changes—they eliminate famine, war, and crime, eventually ushering in a utopia. The humans don't know what the Overlords' ultimate objective is, but later it becomes clear that they're trying to prompt an evolutionary leap in the human race—a leap that the Overlords themselves cannot make because although they're technologically superior, they're otherwise limited: "Despite all their powers and their brilliance, the Overlords were trapped in some evolutionary cul-de-sac. Here was a great and noble race, in almost every way superior to mankind; yet it had no future, and was aware of it."

Evolutionary cul-de-sac. That was how I thought of the streets of Kalamazoo. There were a lot of good things about Kalamazoo, and even some great things, like my family. But I'd already lived 19 years of my life there, which was too long to spend in any one place. And when I went to the grocery store or to work, I ran into people who'd known me since I was a kid, and most of them still applied their old knowledge of me. Even though everything was different now, it was hard to escape the powerful orbit of history, the inertia of the past.

On the porch on New Year's Day, 2008, I made one resolution: to move.

I needed to leave Kalamazoo. I needed to continue evolving. Although I'd moved many times, I knew this wouldn't be like any of the other moves I'd made given the symbolic weight of leaving home for the second time; I'd never thought I'd do it more than once. How much harder things had gotten, how much higher the stakes were compared to when I left home last time, at 18. In May, I'd be turning 30.

After it got dark and the snow settled over the bare limbs of trees and I moved in from the porch to the computer and started an all-out blitz, searching for jobs and sending my resume to schools and organizations from California to Cairo. By my 30th birthday, I'd have a job and I'd be moving—the promise of evolution would be palpable.

I sent out at least a dozen applications a week, waiting for the tiniest nudge in any direction. None came.

Toward the middle of February, we started reading *Childhood's End* in the science fiction class. The line that echoed ceaselessly in my mind was a directive from the Overlords to the humans: "The stars are not for man." As I applied for job after job, it seemed I was sending my CVs straight into a black hole—most of the time I didn't even get the courtesy of a rejection; I was simply ignored. I kept thinking, is this what the universe is telling me, that the vast expanse out there isn't for me?

One afternoon I was exercising at the same YMCA

where my dad had swum a mile a day for over 30 years. An older man whom I'd seen many times over the last year and a half approached me as I paused between sets on a pullover machine.

"You have a big forehead," he said in a matter-of-fact Southern drawl. "What do you do?"

No one had ever introduced himself to me this way before. "I teach," I said, amused. "In fact, I just came from teaching a science fiction class."

And he said, "Have you ever read *Childhood's End*?"

I arched my eyebrow, stared him down a little bit. He waited patiently for my answer, his mouth already fixing to smile. "I'm teaching it right now, as a matter of fact."

The man grinned and introduced himself as Tom Warner, retired astrophysicist and avid science fiction reader.

We became fast friends. He'd leave articles on quantum physics, asteroids, and multiverses tucked behind all the tabloids in the magazine rack where only I would know to look. I'd read them and then we'd talk things over, gabbing breathlessly about everything from science fiction to the presidential election to poetry.

One day he came over to me as I was on the elliptical machine. "Have you ever heard of dark energy?" Tom asked when I took off my headphones.

"It sounds vaguely familiar, but I can't say I know exactly what it is," I said cautiously. Tom often launched into explanations of scientific principles that were immediately, and sometimes embarrassingly, over my head.

Tom nodded. "So the universe is expanding, right?"

"Right," I said. So far so good.

"And it's always been expanding. That's what the universe does. And like everything else, the universe is subject to gravity, so that expansion would naturally slow down over time, right?"

I blinked the sweat from my eyes and tried to concentrate on what he was saying. "The universe would expand more slowly over time because it's getting bigger and heavier. Makes sense to me," I said.

"Exactly. But," he said, pausing for effect, putting a hand on the StairMaster next to me, "it turns out that the universe is actually expanding faster and faster—much more so than it was a long time ago."

"Interesting," I said, not entirely sure what to make of this information.

"The universe is supposed to behave in accordance with certain laws that we have come to hold as incontrovertibly true. Yet here we are with the fact that the universe's expansion is *accelerating*. How is that possible?" Tom's eyes twinkled.

Most of the time I went to the gym because I didn't want to be in my head; I wasn't looking for complicated conversations or thoughts. But I never entertained the idea of shutting Tom down. The fact that there was something he really wanted to tell me, even if it was beyond my grasp, was validating on a level I didn't quite comprehend. "I have no idea how that's possible," I said, and waited for him to tell me something I wouldn't understand.

"The truth is that we don't know why the universe is expanding faster now. The most likely explanation—Einstein's—is that there is some other kind of matter out there that we never knew existed. Dark energy is what we call that theoretical matter or whatever is making the universe do this."

"Okay," I said.

"Or," he said, "maybe it's God."

"I don't think so," I said, a bit startled.

"If the answer doesn't come from science, where else do you think people will look for it? What else could expand the universe at will?" Tom said.

I took a few long gulps from my water bottle, barely

noticing the mechanical movements of my arms and legs. "Well, Arthur Clarke's first law of prediction is that 'Any sufficiently advanced technology is indistinguishable from magic.' The word 'magic' opens the doors to everything, including the spiritual and the supernatural."

"Avenues that science doesn't particularly encourage us to explore," Tom said.

I mopped the sweat from my forehead, glancing down at the console and realizing I'd gone longer than my intended 45 minutes. "Good thing we've got science fiction," I said, the wheels in my head turning.

* * *

I picked up from my dad the habit of keeping the television on in the background. As I worked on job applications, I played episode after episode of *Babylon 5*, a science fiction television show from the 1990s inspired, at least in part, by *Childhood's End*. In the weeks before Dad died, we watched it together. He was immediately captivated by the politics and complexities of operating a space station designed to keep peace between alien races. We only got halfway through season one. At one point soon after Dad's death, I found myself unspeakably upset at the prospect that he'd never get to see the greatest episodes and that he'd never know how the *Babylon 5* story turned out. As I edited, printed and emailed cover letters and resumes, it occurred to me that he wouldn't know how my story turned out, either.

A few weeks later, I was on the Stairmaster sweating mightily, climbing toward some unreachable peak when Tom walked over. "I just read an article in the *Western Herald* about your dad," he said. "I'm sorry." Tom asked me how Dad died, how old he was, whether or not there had been any genetic or lifestyle predictors for his cancer. We talked about cancer as an intelligent and evolving life form that learns to resist and then beat its opposition, with an uncanny use of science fiction battle tactics.

Underneath that conversation was subtext: it had become clear to both of us why our friendship was so important, particularly to me, and what roles we filled for one another. Also, there was the subtext of Tom's mortality—he was older than Dad was when he died. That wasn't lost on either of us, and Tom undoubtedly reflected on his own mortality and the impact it would have on his family.

After a few minutes, Tom lapsed into silence and stared at the oscillating fan on the wall. "At some point, medical science will devise a cancer cure or vaccine of sorts. And this will be great. But I can't help feeling the limitations of something like that, especially given cancer's ability to mutate and learn. A shot seems…I don't know, like spraying air freshener in a garbage dump."

I think about this for a minute. "Are you saying that we need a…spiritual cure?" I asked, chugging up the stairs, looking at him.

"I realize how that sounds," Tom said. "But think about it. Your dad didn't smoke or drink, he exercised, he wasn't genetically predisposed. One concludes then that there was no reason he got sick, other than blind, bad luck. But perhaps there is a reason or some kind of causal link, but it's something we can't see or access. Maybe it's in another dimension, even. Especially given cancer's ability to adapt and evolve, it makes sense that it works in ways we don't or can't fully understand."

Tom never met my dad, yet here he was asking himself the same question I'd been asking myself for the last year and a half. Part of me wanted to avoid that question, as I'd only recently stopped beating myself up about it on a daily basis, but it felt safe to have this conversation with Tom, as though his participation would save me from the punishing endless loop. "One thing that really struck me about my dad's experience," I said, "was how the oncologist—the expert—was baffled at every turn. When the chemo worked, he was surprised; he was even more surprised when it stopped working. When the cancer started spreading again, he was shocked. Every guess he made, every probability and statistic he cited was ultimately meaningless. And it's not because he's a bad doctor— it's because this thing he was trying to predict and treat and defeat was an alien life form, complete with its own rules."

"How little we really know about ourselves," he said. "Regardless of my boundless lack of under-standing, I have faith in the way things work. I have faith that they do work," he said.

I wiped my face with a towel. I wasn't sure I agreed.

"After all, what's the likelihood of you and me becoming friends?" Tom asked.

I smiled. "You have a point there," I said.

* * *

On March 19, 2008, Arthur Clarke died. I saw Tom in the parking lot of the YMCA and he gave a sad salute and put his head down as he walked past. We had a moment of silence at the beginning of class, and then we talked about Clarke's spirit, his soul, whether any part of him existed anywhere. We all agreed that it was possible—that we'd heard crazier things—that there was a realm, maybe many of them, between life and death, interstitial spaces where Clarke or anyone no longer in his earthly phase of existence could dwell, neither alive nor dead, in some form unrecognizable or inconceivable to us. If such places or dimensions existed, we all agreed, then surely someone like Arthur Clarke would dwell there, uncategorized and uncategorizable, defying nothingness.

The afternoon Arthur Clarke died, I spun around slowly in Dad's desk chair. The shelves were almost empty; all the books were now in the department library. I hadn't yet taken down the pictures that crowded the walls—pictures I'd totally forgotten about because they weren't the ones in the hallway of my parents' house or in the albums, pictures that showed us the way my dad saw us: backlit against a campfire on a Northern Michigan campground, laughing mid-bite at the picnic table, stuffing our faces with chocolate while dressed in soggy costumes, crinkling our noses in concentration and disgust while trying to put a writhing worm on a fishing hook. The family on the wall seemed strangely new to me, innocent and sparkling, as though it could have come with the frames.

I continued emptying Dad's desk and file drawers,

skimming quickly through the folders and papers for anything that seemed important and recycling the rest. In the third drawer of Dad's smaller desk, I found myself suddenly sifting through a stack of my own poems. I read them all, slowly, as though I'd never seen them before. If I concentrated, if I pushed my brain back through the quicksand of time, I could picture who I had been when I wrote them. I felt as if that person was gone—dead, even, like the family on the wall, smiling like fools. We had all become ghosts, haunting any space still open to the past.

The symbolism of Clarke's death felt oppressive, an omen clouding the future. The death of a visionary felt to me like the death of a vision—the death of my vision. As I trudged back to my office, my daily routine and the currency of my life seemed more earthbound than ever. I'd expected the job search to be rough, but I hadn't expected to be still entirely unacknowledged almost four months into the process. Unless I pulled a place out of the air and went there on a wing and a prayer, I might not go anywhere at all. Come late May, contracts for the next academic year would arrive; what if I signed one after the other after the other? I thought ahead in time, 5 years, 10, 20, and envisioned myself unlocking the door of Friedmann Hall's third floor and entering the same hallway that smelled of sneakers and Wite-Out and microwave popcorn. A universe folding under its own weight.

In the next few days, I found myself thinking a lot about being stuck. *Babylon 5* underscored my thoughts as the episodes focused on an impending interstellar showdown between two ancient and incredibly powerful alien races who embraced opposite ideologies. Completely outmatched by both sides, the humans, and most of the other races, found themselves caught in the middle of this war. The humans tried to devise a way out of the situation before they and everyone else were obliterated in the cross-fire, but every idea led nowhere, and every attempt failed. It seemed as though the fate of all of these races was out of their hands—every option seemed to lead to destruction.

As May approached, so did my birthday. Kalamazoo was the last place I'd expected to be when I turned 30. No matter where I was I'd have tried not to measure my life against the usual 30-year benchmarks: having a husband and/or kids, a home, a career, a firm establishment in adulthood, in personhood. Being happy. But I was still scraping and scrabbling for my identity, cobbling it together out of various and often fleeting successes, and more frequently, flailings and failures. I still had no leads on a job or a new place to live, no indications of the change that I'd been pursuing with increasingly frantic abandon. Was it okay that at age 30, I had no idea what I was doing or where I was going, that I felt like a lost child loosed upon the world? Even though I was back at the starting point of my personal history, I felt way off the map.

My thirtieth birthday wasn't something I wanted to celebrate. No parties, no cake, no singing. I loaded up my car and drove a few hours to a cabin in the middle of the woods, even though I knew escape was impossible—that my life and all the things I wanted to leave behind would find me in the end, no matter how many stars I sought refuge under.

The night of my birthday, I sat on a rock and looked up into the Big Dipper, into the face of the moon. I closed my eyes and tried to summon my dad, but the echo in my head was louder than if I shouted into a chasm; the words bounced back, illuminating nothing. I started a letter to my dad about how I didn't want to cross into a new decade without him, how I didn't want to be 30 and I didn't want to be an adult. I wanted to be a kid—his kid. I didn't finish that letter. There were no words for what I wanted to say.

I shivered under my birthday moon and pulled the drawstrings of my hood until it was a small circle around my face. I thought about life, about how the here and now, this body, the earth, were infinitesimal, grains, blips, and blinks across an infinite expanse of space and time. My dad and I were both there in that expanse—we always had been and we always would be, along with everything else. The grand, the tragic, the revolutionary—all of it was there.

I thought about the evolutionary trajectory of species in *Childhood's End*—how sentient races, if they had the ability, eventually evolved to a transcendent state in which they could access an infinite consciousness, the "absolute reality" that is the essence of all things—the Brahman. When they did, they transcended reason, corporeality, the brain, time, space, and the universe itself. Clarke fused spirituality with science fiction, which some might find strange or even incompatible, but which made perfect sense to me as I sat under the sky, thirty years old and utterly alone, yet also undeniably part of this universe of constellations and memories and tiptoeing spirits. Clarke was all about granting access; he left room in science, in space, and in stories for mystical, magical, and faith-based elements and entities. *Childhood's End* allowed me the opportunity to consider Dad and to consider myself in a greater evolutionary context, and in so doing, to gain hope that something, however intangible, existed beyond all of this.

In 1999, Arthur Clarke gave a clipping of his hair to a company that sent capsules containing hair samples into space. Clarke's hair eventually took a three-week suborbital ride to space and then returned, ready for another mission—perhaps a longer, more permanent one. Clarke's DNA has and will travel to places that he wrote about; theoretically, an advanced alien civilization could reconstruct his genetic code. Either way, the stuff of Arthur Clarke could exist indefinitely and infinitely. The idea that one's DNA can be perpetuated far beyond one's physical body comforts me and prompts me to continue thinking about what it means that I've felt Dad's presence, sometimes uncannily, on many occasions since his death.

What if life and death as we (think we) know them are only two stages of existing? What if people or spirits or essences can exist in an infinite number of forms not limited to corporeality or to conventional conceptions of an afterlife? Between what we think of as life and death, I imagine countless planes of existence or levels of consciousness or perhaps even dimensions. What if there are actually 7 dimensions, or 11, or 28, and what if some of them are places or spaces we go when we die, or transcend? What if Dad is still here, unrecognizably lingering in interstitial spaces? What if the sense that he's around me isn't just me unable to accept that he's truly gone—what if it's me sensing his particle waves, the way one senses that a radio is on in an adjacent room?

All of this made me think, as I passed into my third decade, that perhaps the stars were not meant for man, or for me—at least, not in my current incarnation. If man could evolve into something not dictated or guided by laws or physiology or DNA, then perhaps he could reach the stars after all. Perhaps I could, too.

* * *

After my birthday, knowing that I had only a couple of weeks before teaching contracts came out for the next year, I redoubled my efforts to move. I start applying for part-time jobs, adjunct positions, even temporary work—anything that might catalyze movement. I played eeny-meeny-miny-moe with cities, trolling for jobs in places toward which I felt the slightest draw, such as Portland and Denver; I flirted with Raleigh, Charlotte, and Asheville, and countless cities across New England. I'd sit at my computer and think, sure, I'd live in Boise! Why not?

I hear Kansas City is really taking off. Madison! Atlanta! I sent applications everywhere, speeding them off with a whisper of good graces. Presuming I could take care of the "if," I'd let the universe decide where.

The next time I saw Tom Warner at the YMCA, he asked how the job search was going. Huffing and sweating up the inclined treadmill, I recapped the last couple weeks, the never-ending flurry of resumes, the consistent lack of response.

Tom nodded thoughtfully, avoiding the usual platitudes, the slap on the back, the "oh, you'll make it happen," which I found increasingly more irritating than supportive.

"Pretty soon I'm going to have to make peace with the idea of being here for another year," I said out loud for the first time. "I'm going to have to figure out some way to be okay—or more than okay—with that. I mean, it's not the end of the world."

We looked at each other; we both knew that it kind of was, at least for me.

After a minute, Tom said, "You probably know this already, but Arthur Clarke's third law is: 'When a distinguished but elderly scientist states that something is possible, he is almost certainly right. When he states that something is impossible, he is probably wrong.'"

I smiled. "Arthur Clarke always manages to say the right thing," I said. "And so do you."

"So take it from a couple of elderly but distinguished scientists," he said. "Don't resign yourself to anything. There's always a work-around. You just have to find it."

* * *

I thought a lot about work-arounds in the following days, and once again my thoughts were uncannily reflected by the episodes of *Babylon 5* running in the background. Ultimately, the humans reject both of the ancient races' ideologies—they reject all the choices offered them and all the options they previously thought possible. They employ a strategy that involves not just inventing new rules, but redesigning the playing field and creating an entirely new game. The warring races abandon them to their new destinies. Upon watching the ships turn away, the commander of the Babylon 5 station says, "the giants have left the playground" and he grins into the vast expanse of space, a child turned into an adult, having just inherited a world of infinite possibility.

The giant has left the playground; in a sense, this was what Dad's death meant. I just hadn't been looking at the world he left behind as a playground—I'd been looking at it as a wasteland. His death had thrust me into undeniable, irrevocable adulthood, into leadership and responsibility the likes of which I'd never known before. I had become things I hadn't asked to be, that I would never have chosen for myself: a caretaker, a custodian of information I didn't want to possess, a watcher of death. But because of these, I also became something I'd had no need to become before—the architect and guardian of hope.

If the universe gives us what we need, rather than what we want, then the story of my life—or at least my perspective on that story—changes. I hadn't been in Vancouver to write my novel or to build a life I would live happily for years to come, or even to attend graduate school. I'd been there because I needed a place from which to be summoned suddenly one sunny day. There had to be a place where the moment that changed everything happened. There had to be a place to leave, a life to leave, a me to leave in order to go back to Kalamazoo.

I had to go back to Kalamazoo—under the circumstances, I wouldn't and couldn't have had it any other way. But I also needed a safe place to test the joints and mortar of my reassembly, to see how much they could hold. And there had to be a Kalamazoo to leave in order for me to continue rebuilding and evolving. There had to be a time and place for me to consciously decide to make my life about something other than Dad's death.

* * *

On May 23rd, I got an email from Emerson College in Boston about a part-time, single-semester teaching gig. That day, I bought a plane ticket to Boston and sent my resume to every college and high school in the city. Ten days later, I flew to Boston and spent five days lugging a suitcase to job interviews and to apartment showings. I decided that even though I'd have to wait to hear about the jobs, I would go ahead and find a place to live. I decided to put all my eggs in that basket. One doesn't make it to the stars by playing it safe.

I slept poorly, sweltering in insomnia on a different couch every night, willing myself the mental and physical stamina to nail job interviews and to navigate the city's housing situation. I thought about how excited Dad would be at the prospect of my moving to Boston—he had taken us there on a family vacation when I was nine. I allowed myself a brief fantasy of walking down Massachusetts Avenue with him, past Harvard and MIT, pausing on the bridge to look at the sun glinting off the State House, to appreciate the rising lights of the city. Whatever place I next inhabited wouldn't know my dad—he would never visit me here.

I also felt curiously liberated; for the first time since he died I felt like a real person—a free person with hopes and dreams and a future that made my stomach buzz with excitement. Was it possible that after all this time dizzying myself with the unanswerable why, Dad's death could take on meaning if I looked at it as a catalyst for evolution?

Childhood's End depicts the evolution of children beyond their parents into something beyond human. Of course, my evolution wouldn't be that dramatic, but I had the distinct sense of being catapulted beyond my parents, especially my dad. And ultimately, wasn't that the point? Weren't predecessors supposed to pave the way for substantial movement, for progress? In *Childhood's End*, the children far surpass their parents; they transcend earthly reality and the traditional notions and confines of humanity itself to join the infinite consciousness. I hadn't merged with the Brahman, but I had outgrown what I was, or what I thought I was. That person no longer existed.

* * *

A few weeks later I was packing up to move to Boston, where an apartment and three part-time jobs waited for me. As I decided what to take and what to leave behind, life swirled about in a surreal haze—I was on my way to living somewhere else, doing something else, being someone else.

The day before I moved, I finished cleaning out Dad's office. I boxed up the rest of the pictures on the walls, scraped the stickers off his door, and slid the nameplate out of the holder and put it in my pocket. I left the key in the lock and the door open. The empty office seemed not to belong to this world, or to any other, as though it was a place in limbo, waiting to be filled. It wasn't clinging to my dad, his belongings, or his memory. It was time for Dad to inhabit some other place, and it was time for me to do the same.

My brother and I installed a hitch on my Chevy Malibu to attach the U-haul trailer that would carry the pieces of my life. My car, smaller and less powerful than recommended to pull such a load, strained like an old horse, topping out at 50 mph. Our set-up felt precarious; again and again I caught myself holding my breath and had to force myself to breathe. The coupler from the hitch to the trailer scraped against the ground every time we hit a bump or drove over an incline, my bike flapped against the back of the car, and my cat buried herself under a blanket.

We talked about stopping along the way and bunking down for some rest, but we decided to press on. A long, exhausting drive felt appropriate. 22 hours later, at 5:30 on a Friday afternoon, we entered the city and immediately got caught in Harvard Square traffic where it became impossible to change lanes with a trailer and people honked at us as if we were trying to land a spaceship on the road. My small car limped and lugged along, the coupling scraping against the ground every few seconds. Every time it did, I cringed and my brother laughed, and I eventually joined him, both of us laughing as we finally pulled up to the house. A policeman came around and instead of hassling me about parking without a permit, held out his hand and with a thick Boston accent welcomed me to the city.

* * *

Arthur Clarke's second law is: "The only way of discovering the limits of the possible is to venture a little way past them into the impossible." I believe this law formed and will continue to form the universe, and support its infinite expansion. I believe this law will support my infinite expansion as well, beyond space and time, beyond my earthly body, beyond my earthly mind. I believe existence doesn't end—it merely moves and changes and takes different shapes and residences, all of which are accessible to me if I know how and where to look.

On Wednesday nights at the Boston University observatory, I look through telescopes at Venus, Mars, and sometimes Jupiter and Saturn. I imagine Arthur Clarke's DNA on its endless voyage, and as I look at our solar system, a relatively tiny parcel of space and land, I realize that in the grand scheme of things, time and space have only as much sway as I allow them. They, like everything else, can be modified and adapted. Arthur Clarke is right—death can beget life, extinction can be evolution: "There lay the Overmind, whatever it might be, bearing the same relation to man as man bore to amoeba...Now it had drawn into its being everything the human race had ever achieved. This was not tragedy, but fulfillment." In this universe, there is room for a million of me—the me that is six years old, still sitting on my dad's knee. The me that tangles with the transition between life and death and back again, between then and now. The me that believes that the three dimensions are only the beginning.

James Miller, for everything; Kate Leary, for being the best manuscript doctor and friend a writer could ask for; Elizabeth Keenan, for priceless advice and support; my friends—you know who you are—for getting sad and angry on my behalf and for pulling me up; Eric Fell, for making me laugh when the world was ending; Zola, for being my only friend in the world sometimes; Sam Deese, for introducing me to Pelekinesis; Mark Givens, for breathing new life into the project; Andreas Schroeder, for encouraging me to write the truth; the travelers I've met along the way—even if I don't remember your names, you changed me; Ray Bradbury, for saving me; and to my family, especially Ola, Bobbi, and Dan, without whom there would be no story.

CPSIA information can be obtained at www.ICGtesting.com
Printed in the USA
BVOW05s0449240615

405501BV00001B/1/P